ENGLISH MEN OF LETTERS

EDITED BY JOHN MORLEY

SIR THOMAS BROWNE

ENGLISH MEN OF LETTERS

SIR THOMAS BROWNE

BY

EDMUND GOSSE

GREENWOOD PRESS, PUBLISHERS
WESTPORT, CONNECTICUT

Originally published in 1905
by The Macmillan Co., New York

First Greenwood Reprinting 1970

Library of Congress Catalogue Card Number 75-98837

SBN 8371-2952-4

PRINTED IN UNITED STATES OF AMERICA

PREFATORY NOTE

SIR THOMAS BROWNE has been particularly fortunate
in his editors, but there are two among them whose
names can never be mentioned by his admirers without gratitude. Each had something of the spirit and
the temperament of Browne himself. Simon Wilkin
(1790–1862) was a paper-maker and then a printer in
Norwich. His tastes were those of a naturalist and
an antiquary, and about 1823 he was attracted to the
writings of the great local celebrity. He found them
in confusion, and he presently began to entertain the
idea of collecting and editing them. This task, in
the course of twelve years, he accomplished with the
help of Thomas Amyot (1775–1850), another enthusiastic Norwich antiquary. Wilkin's edition, in four
volumes, appeared in 1835–36, and few English classics
have been more admirably presented to the public.

The other great benefactor to the lovers of Sir
Thomas Browne is William Alexander Greenhill (1814–
1894), who was a physician and a scholar, like Browne
himself. Greenhill, an Oxford man, who had been the
friend of Newman and Clough, Jowett and Stanley,
settled at Hastings in 1851, and soon afterwards began
to devote himself to the elucidation of Browne's text.

v

For this kind of work he had nothing less than genius.
He worked very slowly, and it was not until 1881 that
he produced his first instalment, containing *Religio
Medici, A Letter to a Friend,* and *Christian Morals.* He
went on steadily, but had not quite finished *Urn-
Burial* and *The Garden of Cyrus* at the time of his
death; these were, however, completed by Mr. E. H.
Marshall, and published in 1896. Although Greenhill's
annotations cover only a portion of Browne's works,
their sagacity and fulness make them, so far as they
go, not merely valuable but indispensable. It is
much to be regretted that Greenhill did not survive
to perform the same office for the *Vulgar Errors* and
for Browne's *Correspondence.*

Several learned friends have obliged me with tech-
nical information in the course of this little mono-
graph. Acknowledgment is made in due course to
Sir Archibald Geikie, to Dr. Norman Moore, and to
Dr. John Peile, Master of Christ's College, Cambridge.
The zoological pages have undergone the revision of
Dr. P. Chalmers Mitchell. Mr. James Fitzmaurice-
Kelly has read the proofs throughout, to their sub-
stantial advantage. For all this kindness I tender,
once more, my warmest thanks.

E. G.

JUNE, 1905.

CONTENTS

SIR THOMAS BROWNE

CHAPTER I

EARLY YEARS: 1605–1641

A NORFOLK antiquary, Peter Le Neve, who became Norroy King-at-Arms, has preserved for us such notes of the pedigree of Sir Thomas Browne as were interesting to himself in his capacity of professional herald. It is probable that Le Neve, who was twenty-one when Browne died, was personally acquainted with him, but, in any case, as one of the glories of Norwich, he found the physician an attractive object. Le Neve was not a writer, but a collector of anti-quarian material. In our present case we have to thank him for a pedigree which he apparently drew up, as part of the history of Norwich, soon after he was made Rouge Croix Pursuivant in 1689. Memories of Browne were then still fresh, and many of his children alive. From this document, supplemented by later investigation,[1] we learn that Sir Thomas descended from a family of Cheshire squires who had resided at Upton for four generations at least before his own; they were entitled to bear arms, and had

[1] Mr. Charles Williams has summed up all that has been dis-covered about *The Pedigree of Sir Thomas Browne* in a privately printed pamphlet which he has courteously sent me. This seems to reach the limit of attainable knowledge.

1

married into good Cheshire families. It is vaguely
stated that the physician's father "was very nearly
related to the Countess of Devonshire," by whom I
suppose that Anne Keighley may be intended. Sir
Thomas Browne himself drew up a short pedigree
of his family in 1663. He shows himself to have
been no herald, and, what is very extraordinary, his
account is full of mistakes. A man may forget the
Christian name of his grandfather and the birthplace
of his mother, but he ought to recollect the birth of
his eldest daughter and be correct as to the ages and
order of his sons. Perhaps Browne thought, in his
own words, that "these are niceties which become not
those who peruse a serious mystery." Rouge Croix,
fortunately, took the matter up more gravely.

The father of Sir Thomas Browne,[1] who bore the
same name as his illustrious son, was the third of the
nine children of that Thomas Browne of Upton whose
name his grandson erroneously believed to have been
Richard. He himself was a mercer in the parish of
St. Michael-le-Quern, in the city of London, and he
married Anne, daughter of Paul Garraway, of Lewes,
in Sussex. She may have been a niece of Sir Henry
Garraway, afterwards Lord Mayor of London. Young
Thomas seems to have been the object of a fond ceremony in his childhood, for his daughter, Mrs. Lyttleton,
records, from family report, that "his father used to
open his breast when he was asleep, and kiss it in

---

[1] The spelling *Brown* must be looked upon as an alternative,
not as an error. On more than one title printed in his life-time he
is named Thomas "Brown," and on the title-page of the folio
Works of 1686, where, if ever, the correct form is to be expected,
we find the author styled "Sr Thomas Brown Kt."

prayers over him, as 'tis said of Origen's father, that
the Holy Ghost would take possession there." The
only other trace of Browne's infancy which can be
gathered refers to his maternal grandfather. He
wrote, in the last year of his life, "I remember, when
I was very young, and, I think, but in coats, my
mother carried me to my grandfather Garraway's
house in Lewes. I retain only in my mind the idea
of some rooms of the house, and of the church." The
Cheshire estates passed to the elder brother of the
mercer, Richard Browne of Upton, and Thomas, it is
evident, had gone up to London to make his own
living, by trade. From his marriage with Anne
Garraway he had four children, of whom the illustrious physician was the youngest.

THOMAS BROWNE was born in the parish of "St.
Michaels Cheap" — as St. Michael-le-Quern, Cheapside,
was commonly called — on the 19th of October 1605.
The first decade of the seventeenth century was not
very rich in the births of literary men. Randolph was
born a few months earlier than Browne; Chilling-
worth three years earlier; the next four years saw
the successive births of Davenant, Waller, Milton,
and Clarendon. These very incongruous names may
help to suggest to us the disparate intellectual elements which were to be characteristic of English
thought during Browne's life-time. The mercer of
Cheapside died early, but in what year is not recorded;
when young Thomas was nineteen the head of the
family, Richard Browne of Upton, also died, and this
may account for the neglect of which we hear. Sir
Thomas's first biographer assures us, we know not on
what authority, that, " according to the common fate of

orphans, he was defrauded by one of his guardians," his
fortune at his father's death having been two-thirds of
£9000. His widowed mother soon married Sir Thomas
Dutton, of Gloucester and Isleworth, who "enjoyed an
honourable post in the Government of Ireland." The
statement of Johnson that Browne was "left to the
rapacity of his guardian, deprived now of both his
parents, and therefore helpless and unprotected," has
always been accepted, although it is only supported by
a much milder statement of Whitefoot's. If Lady Dutton took her widow's third, there were left £6000, not
for Thomas alone, but for her four children. Thomas
was well educated and able to travel freely; if his
mother abandoned him, and his guardian defrauded him
of the greater part of his £1500, it is difficult to know
what were his sources of income. Moreover, there is
evidence that he remained on intimately friendly terms
with his step-father until the death of the latter in 1634.
If the Paul Garraway who died in 1620 was Thomas
Browne's grandfather, it is possible that the boy, who
was then at Winchester, profited by the distribution of
his wealth. All must be left to conjecture, but there
is certainly no evidence of poverty.

Of the youth of Thomas Browne, unhappily, no
particulars have been preserved beyond the bare fact
that he was admitted to a scholarship at Winchester,
on the 20th of August 1616, and that he proceeded
six years later to Oxford, where, early in 1623, he
matriculated as a fellow-commoner of Broadgates Hall,
the name by which what became Pembroke College
during Browne's stay at Oxford was originally known.
It appears, also, that Thomas Lushington, afterwards
a distinguished divine, but then a young graduate

of Lincoln College, was his tutor. That Browne
was distinguished early for his learning appears from
an expression of Anthony à Wood, while Dr. Johnson,
proud of his own connection with Pembroke, and
having remarked that Browne was the first man of
eminence graduated from the new college, characteris-
tically continues, "to which the zeal or gratitude of
those that love it most can wish little better than that
it may long proceed as it began." Browne's taking the
degree of bachelor, the event thus enthusiastically
referred to, occurred on the 30th of June 1626, and
he proceeded master on the 11th of June 1629.

It was probably between these last two dates that
Thomas Browne accompanied his step-father, Sir
Thomas Dutton, to Ireland. Dutton seems to have
been a man of unbridled temper, whose "mutinous
and unworthy courage" in the camp before Juliers
had been severely stigmatised in despatches by Sir
Edward Cecil. He, "upon base advantage, hurt Sir
Hatton Cheke, his colonel," and, being challenged to
duel after the campaign was over, he killed Cheke
upon Calais Sands. This was in 1610, but at a much
later date, the turbulent knight, as we have seen,
"enjoyed an honourable post in the government of
Ireland." There may have been a later duel, for an
incident of this kind is believed to have inspired his
step-son with a copy of verses among the Sloane
Manuscripts of which the following alone seem to be
in a coherent form : —

> "Diseases are the arms whereby
> We naturally do fall and die. . . .
> Men, for me, again shall chime
> To Jared's or Methuselah's time ;

> That thread of life the Fates do twine
> Their gentle hands shall clip, not mine.
> O let me never know the cruel
> And heedless villany of duel ;
> Or if I must that fate sustain,
> Let me be Abel, and not Cain."

The poetical value of these verses is not great, but they have the interest not merely of occurring in the earliest specimen of Browne's composition which we possess, but of being curiously characteristic of him as a physician, as a philosopher, and as a passive resister. In attendance upon the fierce Sir Thomas Dutton, young Browne paid a visit to the castles and fortifications of Ireland. This would probably be at the close of 1626, after the rupture with France, when the coast defences were attracting the attention of a special commission of inquiry. At so favourable an age for observation, and under such interesting conditions, it is to be supposed that Browne saw and noted many things, but it cannot be said that this tour of Irish inspection has left much trace upon his writings. He remarks, indeed, that Ireland is free from toads and snakes, but that was notorious; it is a personal touch, however, which assures us that the belief that there are no spiders in Ireland is a vulgar error, since he has seen them there himself. Like many choleric people, it is possible that Sir Thomas Dutton could make himself very pleasant when he was not crossed. The even temper of Browne would seem to have assuaged him, for the report of Dutton long afterwards in the physician's family, was that he had shown himself "a worthy person."

As a boy Thomas Browne had begun to study the

botany of the day, but "had scarcely ever simpled
further than Cheapside." It is understood that he
turned his attention to medicine while he was still at
Oxford, and it is stated that he even practised as a
physician in Oxfordshire. But this seems unlikely, as
he had taken no medical degree, and as the technical
education offered to her students by the university of
Oxford was meagre indeed. It consisted solely of a
little perfunctory reading of Hippocrates and Galen
in the original. There was no hospital at Oxford and
therefore no clinical school; the very study of drugs
and plants was of a primitive character. If Browne
went through the poverty-stricken classes of Oxford
medical teaching, it could only have been to assure
himself of their worthlessness. His writings may be
searched in vain for the slightest sign of loyalty to
Oxford or gratitude for anything she taught him. The
only possible mark of approval is the fact that in 1666
he sent his son ·Edward to Merton. What is most
likely is, that having tested the medical training of
Oxford, and having found it useless, he buried himself
in his books. His extraordinary learning is seen to
be of a kind, and to extend in a direction, which are
never due to teachers but to the original initiative of
the student. Preparing for a long course of study
abroad, Browne would steep his memory in all the
scientific learning of the age, so as to profit without
any loss of time by whatever revelations might await
him in France and Italy.

The general cessation of hostilities made it easy to
travel through Europe in 1630, at all events in the
west and south. There was a revival of trade with the
Biscayan ports, and we may conjecture that Browne

sailed directly to La Rochelle, partly because he speaks
of having visited that town, and partly because he
discusses the difficulty of spending time well on board
great ships, an experience which fits in nowhere else
in his career. We find him at length at Montpellier,
and this seems an excellent opportunity for quoting
the very remarkable passage in which, soon after his
long residence on the Continent, he reviewed his own
attitude towards foreign habits and customs : —

"I have no antipathy, or rather idiosyncracy in diet,
humour, air, anything. I wonder not at the French for their
dishes of frogs, snails, and toadstools, nor at the Jews for
locusts and grasshoppers; but, being among them, make them
my common viands, and I find they agree with my stomach as
well as theirs. I could digest a salad gathered in a churchyard as well as in a garden. I cannot start at the presence
of a serpent, scorpion, lizard, or salamander. At the sight of
a toad or viper, I find in me no desire to take up a stone to
destroy them. I feel not in myself those common antipathies
that I can discover in others; those national repugnances do
not touch me, nor do I behold with prejudice the French,
Italian, Spaniard, or Dutch ; but where I find their actions in
balance with my countrymen's, I honour, love, and embrace
them in the same degree. I was born in the eighth climate,[1]
but seem for to be formed and constellated unto all. I am no
plant that will not prosper out of a garden. All places, all
airs, make unto me one country. I am in England everywhere and under any meridian. I have been shipwrecked,
yet am not enemy to sea or winds. I can study, play, or
sleep in a tempest. In brief, I am averse from nothing. My
conscience would give me the lie if I should say I absolutely
detest or hate any essence but the Devil; or so at least abhor
anything, but that we might come to composition."

_____

[1] That is to say in the eighth degree of latitude: *Anglia sub
climate octavo sita est*, as Moltkius explained in the Latin edition

When Browne arrived at Montpellier, the " fair city, two parasangs from the sea," that its early historians had loved to praise, he found it greatly fallen from its high estate. The proud days were gone by when James I., King of Aragon, had exclaimed in an ecstasy, "Monspessulanus est una de melioribus villis totius mundi!" Already, in the sixteenth century, after Montpellier passed away from the Kings of Majorca, the famous sea-trade was immensely reduced, and the splendid natural harbour of Cette (then called Sette) had grown to be a dangerous rival. Montpellier was hardly to be considered any longer, what it had been since classic days, the main trading-centre of Languedoc, and its commerce had grown to be chiefly local even before its calamities fell upon it. What these last had been, all visitors in the early seventeenth century could see for themselves. The religious war in 1596 had broken and scarred it in every direction, and in 1621, while Browne was at Winchester, the vast suburbs, full of churches and palaces, which extended on all sides of the old town, were demolished, and every building up to the ancient *enceinte* was razed to the ground. It was to a Montpellier that was raw without, and sadly withered and meagre within, that the medical students of the world were still faithfully flocking.

For, if the city and its civic prestige were under a dark cloud of disaster, the great Faculty of Medicine remained untouched. Indeed, the bounty of Louis XIII. had quite recently encouraged it with fresh grants and privileges. It was, as it had been for centuries, one of the ornaments of France. Its history was, in great part, the history of medicine in Europe.

Montpellier had been in constant touch with the Greeks, and then with the Romans, and then with the Arabs, until the fall of Arabic science, when it stepped into the vacant place. As a school of surgery and medicine, it had its limitations in the days when fresh light was streaming in on all sides; some of the windows of thought in Montpellier were shuttered against the sunshine in 1630. Its schools had never been strong in chemistry, and it was not until long after Browne left that any lectures or demonstrations in this subject were given at Montpellier. Nor did any of its professors take a prominent part in that great revolution in the physics and theory of medicine which made the beginning of the seventeenth century so illustrious in Italy. But nowhere else in the world was the new science of botany studied so thoroughly as at Montpellier, whose Royal Garden was the oldest in Europe; this, too, was the medical school where public demonstrations had first been given in anatomy. The basal training in the profession was more thorough at Montpellier than anywhere else in the world, and consequently vast numbers of students met there every year to go through the preliminary course.

In order to proceed to the baccalaureate degree, a residence of three years was necessary. But few of those foreigners who flocked to Montpellier had the intention of making so long a stay. For their convenience, the whole course of medicine commenced and ended within twelve months, which enabled a student to go on for further work to Italy or Holland. The courses always began about October, at which time, in 1630, we may confidently believe that Browne arrived.

There was an old traditional connection between Oxford and Montpellier, and it is to be supposed that the young man was introduced by his teachers at the English University. The intellectual life at Montpellier had been steadily growing more liberal, in spite of the ravages of the religious wars. The Faculty of Medicine was entirely distinct from the university of the town, and from the clerical authorities; it was itself allowed to bear the name of University, and its students were under no regular religious inspection. It had resisted the innovations of Paracelsus, and the temptation to join in any theological disputes; it held that all it gave to its students was the benefit of a practical knowledge of the human body. There had been a reaction against the general Calvinism of an earlier time; but in 1629, the year before Browne's arrival, the laxity of faith persisting among the Montpellier students had led the Jesuits co take charge of such education in Theology as the University of Medicine admitted. But Montpellier was still as tolerant a place as a young Protestant of liberal views could visit.

The students were at that time taught by the six regius professors, all of them men whose salaries were not merely small, but steadily diminishing, and who had to look to the exercise of the profession for their emoluments. The old system of instruction had given place to a mode of teaching which was wholly practical, and which must have resembled that at our great hospitals to-day. The object was to make the student master of the groundwork of his business as a physician or a surgeon, not to fill his mind with miscellaneous scholastic knowledge. It was this severe practical training, enforced by means of tough examinations, which made Montpellier almost indispensable in those days to foreign students, who could get no training like it anywhere else in Europe. We may note that it was Lazare Rivière whose lectures on medicine our student attended. This excellent practitioner, the "Riverius" of Browne's correspondence was professor at Montpellier from 1622 to 1655. His *Praxis Medica*, long the text-book in the schools, unquestionably represents the identical lectures to which the future author of *Religio Medici* listened.

At the time that Browne studied at Montpellier, the school of that faculty taught that the life distributed through the body was due to an organic soul, the "vital principle" of which animated the tissues, and gave warmth and movement to the body. This was the theory of "vitalism" which Descartes rejected; and at a little later date than the time we are discussing, the school of Montpellier was invaded by Cartesian ideas, and the theory of "vitalism" was routed, not without angry controversy. But it is interesting to see that Browne, who imbibed the Montpellier tuition at a tender age, remained somewhat impressed by this notion of the organic soul, which alone makes some passages of his writings still intelligible to us.[1]

From Montpellier, Browne passed on to the famous university of Padua, then esteemed the centre of the world of science. If, as we have every reason to sup-

---

[1] Much in this account of the state of Montpellier in the early part of the seventeenth century has been collected from *Mémoires pour servir à l'Histoire de la Faculté de Médecine de Montpellier*, a posthumous work by the medical antiquary, Jean Astruc (1684–1766). Access to this rare volume I owe to the kindness of my friend, Dr. Norman Moore.

pose, his three years of continental study were equally
divided, we may think of him as in Padua from the
autumn of 1631 to that of 1632. Education was
splendidly endowed in this noble city, which flourished
under the sway of the Venetian State. We are told
that it was considered a dull year in the course of
which more than one thousand new students did not
matriculate at the university. It was in Padua that
for upwards of a century young men from all parts of
Europe had received surgical teaching such as could
nowhere else be supplied. Our own John Caius had
studied there, and had enjoyed the inestimable privi-
lege of lodging for eight months under the roof of the
illustrious Vesalius. It was the genius of this extraordinary man (Andrea Vesale), which had given Italy,
and especially Padua, the pre-eminence in all branches
of surgical and anatomical science during the sixteenth
century. He had started that bold opposition to the
dry doctrine of Galen which appeared at first so scandalous a heresy, and was met by so many cries of
horror. It had been continued by his great disciples,
particularly by Columbo, Eustachio, and Gabriele
Falloppio, all glories of the school of Padua. It was
Realdo Columbo who first vivisected dogs with a view
to the investigation of human maladies, and in later
years Browne seems to have particularly recommended
him as a guide to his own pupils. But Falloppio sur-
passed all his predecessors in the ingenuity of his
discoveries, and he had been succeeded by Girolamo
Fabrizio of Acquapendente, the forerunner and master
of our own Harvey.

Three generations of professors of this intrepid class
had placed Padua easily at the head of European

science. Since the days of Harvey, indeed, who had studied there under Fabrizio from 1598 to 1600, if the school of surgery had not positively declined, it had grown stationary. But physiology and anatomy had not relaxed their efforts; and the most eminent of living surgeons, Pietro Marchetti, had already begun his work there as a teacher, succeeding Spieghel (Spigelius), who had died in 1625. Columbo had said that more was to be learned from one vivisection than from all the writings of Galen; and it was the clinical teaching which still upheld the unrivalled prestige of Padua. Nowhere else in Europe could the progress of disease be studied to such advantage; the students visited the hospitals, and had the symptoms detailed before their eyes. The Venetian Republic protected science against the attacks and insinuations of the Church; and amusing tales were told of such state defiance to fanaticism as could nowhere out of Venice be hoped for. There was an anatomical theatre, a sort of wooden barrack, which could hold an immense concourse of students; this was rebuilt every year, and was one of the sights of the city.

Nor were medicine and botany neglected, though not so prominently encouraged. Browne must have attended the lectures of Sanctoro Sanctorio, the friend of Galileo, and must have argued with his fellow-students about the professor's *Medicina Statica*, then lately published, a work over which Europe was still wrangling. There was a great garden of herbs, oval in shape, of which the Paduans were very proud. This was already under the charge of John Wesling, who lectured in it, and who became a little later on professor of botany. He was still eminent in Padua

when Evelyn visited the city in 1645 and wrote down
in his *Diary* so delightful an account of what he saw.
There can be no doubt that the strenuous intellectual
life of Padua, so different from anything he had ex-
perienced in Oxford, made its life-long impression on
Browne. Everything there was calculated to awaken
a philosophical imagination. The schools of surgery
and medicine, to which his daily labours took him,
were held in the buildings around a great quadrangle,
with columns above, and, underneath, cloisters where
eager students accompanied the professors, and discussed results. The arms of the Venetian Republic
were over the great gate, and the Lion of St. Mark
dominated all. But what we can fancy was most in
sympathy with Browne's habit of mind was the famous
inscription under which every student had to pass, in
going and coming, reminding him that he must so
enter as to become each day more learned than he was
before, and so learn as to be more useful to his father-
land and to the state.

From Padua Browne proceeded northward to the
comparatively new university of Leyden, which had
lately developed educational facilities that made it of
great importance to students of medicine. One advantage of coming to the Dutch university from Italy was
the obtaining of fresh points of view for the observation
of theoretical science. Against the great surgical and
anatomical schools of Montpellier and Padua, it was
urged that they neglected chemistry. There was little
place for it in their curriculum. The physiatric system
of the Italian professors was the complete opposite of
that chemical system which now flourished at Leyden,
under the celebrated Jan Baptista van Helmont, whose

lectures Browne must have attended. Pieter van
Foreest, the earliest professor of medicine in the new
university, had traced the path of the science at Leyden,
where what must have especially interested Browne was
the general enthusiasm for chemical facts. Everything
was leading up towards the system of therapeutics to
be presently developed by the celebrated Sylvius
(Francis de le Boe), with his universal attribution of
disease to acidity, to the presence of acrimonious
fluids in the animal structure. Sylvius, a student of
precocious parts, some years younger than Browne,
must have entered at Leyden while Browne was there.
There was a small infirmary with twelve beds at
Leyden, and this would be serviceable to strangers
like Browne, although it was not until some years later
that Sylvius invented the modern practice of "walking
the hospital," by taking his pupils "by the hand" to
medical practice from bedside to bedside. It is quite
possible that Browne may have met Descartes at
Leyden. The Frenchman went there in 1629, and
though he moved about to Amsterdam and Utrecht,
Leyden was his headquarters till the parsons made it
too uncomfortable for him in 1649. Before Browne
left Leyden, he took his degree of doctor of medicine
there, and soon after, probably in the autumn of 1633,
he returned to England.

We cannot overrate the importance of what the
peculiar temperament of Thomas Browne owed to this
prolonged foreign travel and this con　　　ce with exotic
schools of thought. An ordinary young Englishman,
of insular temper, might take the grand tour in all
its divisions, and return as narrow as he went forth.
But Browne, to a greater extent, perhaps, than any

other man of his generation, was prepared by nature to break the bonds of intellectual convention upon the least possible encouragement. It was therefore of unsurpassed advantage to him that he had, in his riper years and confirmed judgment, seen, as he says, and examined all that the fermenting scientific world of France and Italy and Flanders had to offer of what was curious and new. He was able, without painful effort, to throw off, or to keep from acquiring, the mental prejudices which were typical of the strenuous, straitened English tradition of the early seventeenth century. As a youth, at Montpellier, he had been confronted by those symbols of the Catholic religion which it was so difficult for English Puritans of his class to put up with. But Browne soon learned to take his hat off whenever a cross or crucifix was carried past him in the street. He could not bring himself to laugh at, but was rather constrained to pity, "the fruitless journeys of pilgrims," while "the miserable condition of friars" appealed to his sympathy and not to his scorn. Looking back upon his years in France and Italy, Protestant and Englishman as he was, he has to confess: "I could never hear the Ave-Mary bell without an elevation," and he tells us how careful he always was to avoid wounding the conscience of those around him by "silence and dumb contempt."

In all this Browne was unique in his generation. The behaviour of Englishmen in the Latin countries might certainly be considered courageous, for it often led them into dangerous predicaments, but it was not sympathetic. At Montpellier, the other English students, when they saw a solemn procession pass along the streets, distinguished themselves by "an excess

C

of scorn and laughter." Browne, on these occasions, agitated alike by the emotion of the rite and by sorrow at the prejudice of his fellow-countrymen, had been so much overcome as to "weep abundantly." His peaceable spirit desired to learn rather than to dogmatise; above all, it desired to comprehend and to feel, to distinguish and to penetrate, the genuine sensations of others, not in the temper of a judge but in that of a physician. He had argued with Franciscan monks in France without loss of temper upon either side, and with doctors of physic in Italy, "who could not perfectly believe the immortality of the soul, because Galen seemed to make a doubt thereof." He had observed the singular case of "a divine, and a man of singular parts, who was so plunged and gravelled with three lines of Seneca" that all the antidotes which Browne produced from human and divine philosophy "could not expel the poison of his error." On these, and a thousand other incidents of foreign manners, the heart of the wise youth brooded, and he came to the conclusion that each country hath its Machiavelli, each age its Lucian, and that we ought to try every spirit.

He came back to England in 1633; and in that year the posthumous *Poems* of Dr. Donne were published. To the first edition of this popular work (and to the first edition only) were appended some curious lines signed " Tho : Browne." When the sequence of " Elegies upon the Author " was reprinted, this copy of verses alone was suppressed, and it appears to be unknown to readers of Donne and of Browne. The lines form an apology for those looser writings of his youth which were a scandal to the admirers of the great Dean of

St. Paul's.   In a spirit of great indulgence the youthful
poet tells the ghost of Donne that he feels no inclination
to blame or wonder

> " at this strange fire
> That here is mingled with thy sacrifice,
> But dare read even thy wanton story
> As thy confession, not thy glory."

The ingenuity of excuse, and the moderation which
hates to find fault, seem characteristic of the author of
Religio Medici.   These lines, which have as much or as
little merit as Browne's customary efforts at poetry,
were omitted in later editions of Donne, no doubt
because it was held indiscreet to draw such particular
attention to the divine's " poems of the looser sort."
   It was now, perhaps, that Browne practised physic
for a while in Oxfordshire ; but we find him presently
a resident of Halifax in Yorkshire.   Bentley, writing
during the life-time of Dr. Edward Browne, says that
his father " fixed himself in this populous and rich
trading place, wherein to show his skill and gain
respect in the world : and that during his residence
amongst us, and in his vacant hours, he writ his
admired piece," *Religio Medici*.   Other accounts add
the information that the famous treatise was composed
at Shipden Hall, a house near Halifax.   The entire
absence of documents at this period of Browne's career
is much to be lamented, since, when his private correspondence begins to be preserved, some fifteen years
later, we find him still keeping up old friendships in
Halifax.   We are, however, able to fix with reasonable
exactitude the date at which the *Religio Medici* was
written.   The preface " To the Reader," prefixed to

the first authorised edition, that of 1643, offers us some
precious autobiographical information. It tells us that
the book was composed "about seven years past,"
which would take us back to 1636. But in the first
part of the work itself, Browne says, "as yet I have
not seen one revolution of Saturn, nor hath my pulse
beat thirty years," and, in the second part, " my life,
it is a miracle of thirty years." The first of these
remarks must have been written before the 19th of
October 1635, and the second not long after that
date.

The *Religio Medici* was not composed for the public,
or at least for immediate publication. It was a
"private exercise," a personal record of the adventures
of a questioning spirit. Browne was inactive by inborn disposition; he composed slowly, fitfully, with
alternations of zeal and languor. To deprecate the
charge of egotism he uses an expression which breathes
the very temper of Montaigne. *Religio Medici* is not
to be regarded as a book of philosophical importance ;
it is nothing, he declares, but "a memorial unto *me*."
On that ground he hoped at first to avoid discussion
altogether; the book was to be a confidential document, a sort of private diary of the soul. When we
come to analyse the *Religio Medici*, we shall deal with
it as it was given to the world in 1643. But evidence
is not wanting that Browne's mind had undergone
some changes in those eight years. Since 1635 his
opinions on several matters had become more conservative. Many things, set down in 1635, were
"plausible unto my passed apprehension, which are
not agreeable unto my present self" in 1643.

He has one of his odd terms of phrase, adroitly

excusing anything which may seem excessive in his
early boldness of thought; he begs the reader to consider his expression "tropically" put, that is to say
figuratively, with a free use of rhetorical tropes. We
may do so, of course, if we please, but if we wish to
enter into Browne's mind in its early freshness, we
shall not be wise to explain away, but rather to inten-
sify, his brave outlook upon life. Certainly, as time
went on, he became more timid, more submissive to
authorised judgments. He tells us, and we receive the
confession with regret, that he gradually conquered his
philosophy on his knees. For instance, his difficulty
about miraculous interposition seems to have lessened
in later life, or to have been more resolutely pushed
behind him; while it is a very curious fact that
whereas, in the present text, he declares that (in 1643)
he had "no taint or tincture" of heresy, schism, or
error, the manuscripts and the unauthorised texts repre-
sent him (in 1635) as confessing precisely the reverse,
namely that he is conscious of such a taint or tincture.

Browne wrote his treatise for his own contentment,
and was prepared to allow it to sink into oblivion.
But the friendliest and most companionable of men
could not compose a book so warm-hearted, and not
crave the sympathy of a reader. It was shown first to
one person, and then to another; at length permission
was given to friend after friend to copy, always confidentially, so curious and comfortable a piece. Dr.
Johnson was strangely vexed at the author's relation
of these facts, and in his life of Sir Thomas Browne
he flies out in a passion : —

" A long treatise (he says), however elegant, is not often
copied by mere zeal or curiosity, but may be worn out in

passing from hand to hand, before it is multiplied by a transcript. It is easy to convey an imperfect book, by a distant hand, to the press, and plead the circulation of a false copy as an excuse for publishing the true, or to correct what is found faulty or offensive, and charge the errors on the transcriber's depravations. This is a stratagem, by which an author, panting for fame, and yet afraid of seeming to challenge it, may at once gratify his vanity, and preserve the appearance of modesty."

This is vigorously put, but the attribution of such a stratagem to Sir Thomas Browne is justified neither by external nor internal evidence. If Johnson had been better acquainted with seventeenth-century literature, English as well as French, he would have been familiar with the circumstance that books much longer than *Religio Medici* were often spontaneously multiplied in manuscript.[1] But we are not left to conjecture, since of this particular work at least five manuscripts actually survive, although such transcripts would naturally be destroyed as soon as a printed text was available.   There is no reason whatever to suppose that Browne was "panting for fame." So far from showing any vanity in this performance, he speaks in his *Commonplace Book* of *Religio Medici* as "a piece of mine, published long ago," as though unaware, or at

[1] There are examples in most literatures. Sannazaro's *Arcadia* was actually printed, to his furious indignation, from a manuscript copy during his absence from Italy. Mr. James Fitzmaurice-Kelly is pretty sure that the first part of *Don Quixote* circulated in manuscript; for if not, as he has pointed out, how could Lope de Vega say that it was rubbish, and how could the author of the *Picara Justina* refer to it, before it was published? English students will recall the cases of books far longer than *Religio Medici*, such, for instance, as Sidney's *Arcadia* and Spenser's *Faerie Queene*.

least careless, of all the stir and the admiration it had
awakened. One reason why he might be disinclined
to draw particular attention to it, is one which can
with difficulty be appreciated by a modern reader.
Those who then wrote on serious subjects, however
original or even subversive their ideas might be, were
expected to dignify their argument by copious quota-
tions from the Ancients and from the Fathers. To
appear without one's Latin was to stroll in the street
on a public occasion without one's wig. Browne
laments the lack of a library; there were no good
books — that is to say books which enshrined the
heavy learning of Europe — on his shelves at Shipden
Hall. So Jeremy Taylor, a year or two later, bemoaned
his misfortune at having to write *The Liberty of Pro-
phesying* away from his library. Neither of these
great authors appreciated the immense advantage they
gained from being torn from their traditional support,
and made to depend for their ornament on their imagination and their memory.

In 1637 some Norfolk friends united in urging
Thomas Browne to come over to Norwich to settle
there as a practising doctor. Among them was Mr.
(afterwards Sir) Justinian Lewin, who was a Pembroke
man. To the persuasions of these friends, Browne's
old tutor, Dr. Thomas Lushington, by this time rector of
Burnham Westgate, in Norfolk, added his recommenda-
tion. This move may not have been unconnected with
the fact that, on the 10th of July 1637, Browne was
incorporated a doctor of physic at Oxford, having two
years earlier taken his degree at the London College
of Physicians. Perhaps his reappearance at Pembroke,
and renewed intercourse with old friends who lived in

Norfolk, led to the invitation to Norwich. Thither, at all events, he now proceeded, and immediately took up a professional practice which he continued, with eminent success, until his death forty-five years later.

To close the scanty record of this early portion of Browne's career, it should be said that in 1641 he married Dorothy, the fourth daughter of Edward Mileham, of Burlingham St. Peter. The bride was twenty years of age, the bridegroom thirty-six. This marriage was fortunate to a high degree. Mrs. Browne was "a lady of such symmetrical proportion to her worthy husband, both in the graces of her body and mind, that they seemed to come together by a kind of natural magnetism." So the excellent Whitefoot says, and he had opportunities of observing the couple through the whole of their married life. A few of Dorothy Browne's letters have been preserved; they do greater credit to her sentiments than to her spelling; she liked her "sheus" to be "eythar pinke or blew," and had a partiality for "whight silk" lined with "slit grene sarsanat." She bore ten children, six of whom died before their parents. Save for such bereavements, which were accepted in the seventeenth century with much resignation, the married life of Thomas Browne seems to have been one of unclouded happiness. We leave him prosperously settled in Norwich, "much resorted to for his skill in physic."

CHAPTER II

RELIGIO MEDICI

RELIGIO MEDICI, which to Browne's contemporaries possessed a dangerous savour of scepticism, has come to be considered by us as a work of practical piety. The mind of its author had a curious mixture of directness and tortuousness which disguises from all but the careful reader the singleness of his aim. But those who are persistent in studying the whole of *Religio Medici* — a book far too often treated as if it were a mere storehouse of striking paradoxes — will discover that an unbroken thread runs through it. It lies spread out before us like a smiling champaign, through which, with singular turns and convolutions, undulates a shining river of argument. The casual observer sees the light and the beauty, but there seems to him no current, no fall. Yet, winding as it is, the stream does move, and it descends, with soft regularity, to a goal in the far distance. We must therefore give no excessive attention to Browne's fantastic escapes from the obvious, nor must we be deceived by the caprices of his fancy. His argument, if you give it time and scope, will not lose its way nor miss its appointed aim.

The object of *Religio Medici*, then, when we lay it down after a careful reading, is seen to be a defence

of the attitude of a mind that is scientific and yet
reverent. The subject of the treatise is religion as it
appears, we may almost say on second thoughts, to an
intellect which for a long time past has been concerned
exclusively with natural experiment, and which comes
back to religion habituated to the experimental attitude. The *medicus* is a man, physician or surgeon,
whose business it is by imbuing the human body with
medicines or by performing manual operations on it, to
cure the physical ills to which our race is subject. In
order that he may learn to be able to do this, he has
to give long years of his best attention to material
matters, to a close and untiring examination of the
bodily structure in health and in disease, to drugs and
diet, to a whole circle of experiences which are the
reverse of spiritual. The mind of such a *medicus*,
when it is stored with physical knowledge, will revert
to a consideration of the supernatural, but in a mood
how changed! He knows that his faith has passed
through a fiery trial; " my greener studies have been
polluted," he confesses, with heresies and errors. But
are these to hold their power over his soul ?

Religion, urges the sceptic, is all very well for the
childish, for the inexperienced, for the ignorant. But
how does it affect you, the instructed, the illuminated,
you who come, learned far above your fellows, from
discussion over the sources of life and the causes of
death in the anatomical theatre of Padua? Well,
replies Browne, in his long-drawn, plausible way, that
is exactly what we must find out. We must see how
religion stands the test of a return to it after a thorough
scientific education. The world, he finds, has persuaded
itself that because he has devoted himself so long to

anatomy, he must have no religion. In his smiling can-
dour, he admits that the world has some excuse for its
opinion. If he is expected to pull a long face, and
blaspheme all cakes and ale; if religion necessitates
casting up the whites of one's eyes and denouncing all
men whose opinions differ in measure from one's own,
and sitting in fierce judgment upon one's neighbours,
then Browne has to retire. He has to admit that he
does not conform to the Puritan type. His behaviour
is indifferent; his discourse speculative; his profession suspected; his studies are physical and free. If
religion is incompatible with all this, he must wave his
hand to the churches.

But he is determined not to admit this incom-
patibility; and in his refusal to do so lies his great
originality, and the passionate welcome which was at
once accorded on so many sides to his book. In an
age of theological fury, Browne argued without heat.
His was pre-eminently a peaceable spirit. He had no
pleasure in controversy for its own sake, and he therefore opens his discourse with a series of statements
which are intended to ward off discussion and to
rout suspicion. The opening fact of *Religio Medici* is
that its author insists on being styled a Christian.
Those who are not for us, our Saviour had said, are
against us. Browne, in his subtle way, might have
contested the truth of this position, but he declines to
do so. He accepts it, and he is with the Christians,
not against them. It is very distressing to him that
there should be so much internecine strife among those
who make the same claim as he. But he looks ahead
with a noble foresight, and in spite of the discordant
jarring of the sects conceives " that revolution of time

and the mercies of God" will effect a conciliation
between those who, to an eye fixed upon the miserable
present age, seem as unlikely to be united as the
poles of heaven.

After a general survey, the *medicus* prefers the
Church of England. But he accepts her rule not
because he thinks her infallible, but because, on the
whole, and having examined other systems of piety,
there is no church whose every part so squares into
his conscience. He endeavours to observe her constitutions. But outside the skeleton of her Articles,
he fills up the outlines of his conduct in harmony
with his personal convictions : —

> " Whatsoever is beyond, as points indifferent, I observe
> according to the rules of my private reason, or the humour
> and fashion of my devotion ; neither believing this because
> Luther affirmed it, or disproving that because Calvin hath
> disavouched it. I condemn not all things in the Council of
> Trent, nor approve all in the Synod of Dort. In brief, where
> the Scripture is silent, the Church is my text ; where that
> speaks 'tis but my comment : where there is a joint silence
> of both, I borrow not the rules of my religion from Rome
> or Geneva, but the dictates of my own reason."

This is Thomas Browne's creed, and it is so moderate,
and in essentials so conservative, that we may wonder
that it awakened any scandal. We shall see, however,
later on, what exceptions were made to it, and at what
particular points it was attacked. But returning for
the time being to the *medicus* himself, we presently
detect a cunning in his apparent innocency. It would
not have been worth while for him to compose a long
treatise merely to assert that he is in accordance with
the Church of England. He makes his confession, as

we have seen, rather glibly in order that under the
shelter of it he may insinuate some more subtle re-
servations.   And first of all he explains to us how
decidedly his individual temperament urges him to
take up an attitude of philosophic doubt, how little of
the temper of the dogmatist he possesses : —

"I could never divide myself from any man upon the difference of an opinion, or be angry with his judgment for not
agreeing with me in that from which perhaps within a few
days I should dissent myself. I have no genius to disputes
in religion, and have often thought it wisdom to decline
them, especially upon a disadvantage, or when the cause of
truth might suffer in the weakness of my patronage."

This leads him to a statement, dropped almost as an
aside, which is of the most tremendous importance.
Just as we are wondering where the results of an
experimental education will come in, and in what this
docile, rather indifferent churchman is distinguished
from all the rest of his pious co-parishioners, a voice
whispers, "In philosophy, where truth seems double-
faced, there is no man more paradoxical than myself;
but in divinity I love to keep the road." We have
now the key to Browne's argument, which is that if a
man of science will hold the truth of the Christian
religion sincerely in mystical matters, he may take as
his reward the right to examine the material world of
nature with all the scepticism which his experimental
heart desires. Theology and science in water-tight
compartments, with no possibility of interchange between them, — that is the ideal of the physician's
religion, and that the system upon which he can obey
the Church and yet be absolute monarch of his own
mental processes.   What the Bible declares, although

it may seem to be outside the range of his experience
as a doctor, he will implicitly believe, but he claims
the right to interpret the text as he pleases and to
retreat to his " solitary and retired imagination." The
liberty an instructed man enjoys in the circle of his
own private thoughts was never more splendidly
asserted than by this zealous partisan of Church and
State. On one hand he cries, " *Certum est, quia impossible est*," on the other he seems to echo the noble
protest of our modern poet : —

> " Because man's soul is man's God still,
>   What wind soever waft his will
>   Across the waves of day and night,
>   To port or shipwreck, left or right,
>   By shores and shoals of good and ill;
>   And still its flame at mainmast height
>   Through the rent air that foam-flakes fill
>   Sustains the indomitable light
>   Whence only man hath strength to steer
>   Or helm to handle without fear."

Theology has laid down general laws, but she leaves
to the soul, in the exercise of its sovereign powers, the
intellectual execution of them. Scripture points the
road, but it is the soul, and the soul alone, which can
arrange the details of pedestrian experience. And
here comes in the value of a scientific education, which
gives a man courage and wisdom in deciding all matters
outside the formulas of doctrine. " I perceive every
man's own reason is his best Œdipus," says Browne,
" and will find a way to loose those bonds wherewith
the subtleties of error have enchained our more flexible
and tender judgments."

The position which the *medicus* has now reached is

so interesting that we wish him to persist in it. But
he sees its danger in a fanatic age, and he takes one
of those sudden turns, those convolutions of the stream
of thought, by which he loves to puzzle us. Scarcely
has he asserted the right of man's own soul to be his
guide, than he turns to chatting about heresies, and
seems to resign all that he has gained. He prattles
about errors which he used to hold, — that the soul
might perish and rise again with the body; that all
men shall finally be saved; that we may pray for the
dead. He declares, almost unctuously, that he never
revealed these soul-destroying errors to any of his
dearest friends (although now he reveals them to the
world); he assures us, very volubly, that he has no
pleasure in propaganda, and no wish to found a sect.
We wonder what he is, in vulgar phrase, " driving at,"
till it occurs to us that whenever Browne is particularly chatty, we shall find that he is concealing something of his intentions. The argument, sure enough,
takes another turn, and we see again where we are.

Under cover of the extravagance of his assurance
that he is himself no heretic, he now insinuates the
conviction, alarming enough in the early seventeenth
century, that heresy cannot be extirpated. Under the
guise of a reproof of the habit the Christian churches
have " to mince themselves almost into atoms," he de-
mands a wide liberty of intellectual action for men of
" singular parts and humours." Science has a domain
of her own, where the schools and the councils have
no authority to intrude, " wherein the liberty of an
honest reason may play and expatiate with security,
and far without the circle of an heresy."

The scepticism which has been awakened in the

breast of the physician by his experience in dealing
with the facts of the material world does not, however,
in the case of Thomas Browne, exasperate him to a
general defiance of religious tradition. He accepts
the latter, and he looks about to find a relief from the
mental irritability which arises in his spirit. He finds
it in a contemplation of the incomprehensibility of the
Christian mysteries. Browne's was a meditative nature ;
he was neither a mystic nor a theological metaphysi-
cian, and he early found an immense satisfaction in
resigning to others those " wingy mysteries in divinity "
which exercised the minds of his robust Puritan contemporaries. In a happy hour he discovered that the
visible world is but a portrait of the invisible, and that,
as his genius lay towards physic, not towards meta-
physic, he could safely leave dogma to those who
appreciated it, while he devoted his own energies to
deciphering " the public manuscript of nature." In
other words, his religious feelings were sincere, but he
learned to keep them rigidly apart from his scientific
investigation. He considered it worse than useless
for a man of his temperament to discuss niceties of
theological dogma. The wise plan for the scientific
investigator was to accept the decisions of the Church
with humility, bow the head, and then go on making
physical inquiries without any further reference to
religion.

A delicate prudence was requisite in carrying out
this scheme. It was much more difficult for a
Protestant in England than for a Catholic in France
or Italy to do it. Browne's great contemporary,
Descartes, had just the same horror as our *medicus*
for theological controversy, and he escaped exactly

as Browne did, on the "figurative sense" of Scripture. He, too, was careful to put in conciliatory, ingratiating phrases now and then about the Church, and he found strong backers among the Oratorians and the Jansenists. He put the results of science and religion apart, in separate pigeon-holes, excluding each from communication with the other, but he did it with impunity. Even the Jesuits, with whom alone in a Catholic country the man of science was likely to come into collision, were apt to be indulgent in these matters. They seem, as a rule, to have tolerated discussion of physical conditions, so long as the authority of the Church was not formally impugned.

But the English Puritans were far less tolerant; they looked with grave suspicion on all those who went prying about to unravel the secrets of the physical world. And as the seventeenth century proceeded, in France as well as in England, the tendency was not to liberality but to a sterner formalism. The desire "to live in peace and to continue the course of life he had begun" was Descartes' excuse for suppressing the *Traité du Monde* in 1633, when the condemnation of Galileo had scared him; and, meanwhile, the temper of Port-Royal grew more and more adverse to science, as it appeared to the Jansenists that it encouraged libertinism. We shall have to insist on this when we touch on the extraordinary contrast between Browne and Pascal, whose attitude to science presently led them into paths diametrically opposite. For the moment we need but remind ourselves that the state of social and political confusion in England was directly beneficial to Browne in giving him immunity in his perilous

experiment. In 1643, the zealots had something else
to occupy them than the worrying of an obscure
physician, who loudly declared that he was essentially
in sympathy with their views, and who offered no
objection on any point of doctrine.

Browne proceeds, under shelter of his constant
protests of orthodoxy, to show how divine wisdom
is aided in its exercise by the discoveries of the
medical profession. An address in verse breaks his
arguments here with an invocation of the Deity, and
is worthy of our attention. Browne's poetry is never
very skilful in form, but he uses it to hammer out
thoughts which do not lend themselves to expression
in prose. On the subject of the mission of the man
of science he says : —

" Teach me to soar aloft, yet ever so,
  When near the Sun, to stoop again below ;
  Thus shall my humble feathers safely hover,
  And, though near earth, more than the heav'ns discover ;
  And then at last, when homeward I shall drive,
  Rich with the spoils of nature, to my hive,
  There will I sit like that industrious fly,
  Buzzing Thy praises, which shall never die,
  Till death abrupts me, and succeeding glory
  Bids me go on in a more lasting story."

He prefers the study of little things to that of
big things. The microscope suits his eyes better
than the vast sweep of the telescope. He very
quaintly tells us that he finds no pleasure in looking at whales or elephants or dromedaries; these
prodigious and majestic pieces of Nature's handiwork
appal him by their size. He loves to watch the
habits of bees and ants and spiders, and considers

that "in these narrow engines there is more curious
mathematics, and that the civility of these little
citizens more neatly sets forth the wisdom of their
maker." He continues : —

"I could never content my contemplation with those general
pieces of wonder, the flux and reflux of the sea, the increase
of Nile, the conversion of the needle to the North; and have
studied to match and parallel those in the more obvious and
neglected pieces of Nature, which, without further travel, I
can do in the cosmography of myself. We carry with us
the wonders we seek without us ; there is all Africa and her
prodigies in us. We are that bold and adventurous piece of
Nature [how Browne loves to repeat this phrase!] which he
that studies wisely learns in a compendium what others
labour at in a divided piece and endless volume."

Here speaks the careful naturalist, as we are prepared to find him in the pages of the *Vulgar Errors*,
well content with an intense examination of a narrow
field; well pleased, too, in spite of the attractions of a
great centre like London, to make a little country-
town his home and its parish-bounds the limit of his
ambition. His appeal to a closer and more reverent
study of Nature starts from this modest apprehension
of the value of small things. He urges on the reader
the probability of his finding the Divine purpose more
clearly revealed in the wing of an insect than in the
motions of the heavenly bodies, not because the latter
are less wonderful, but because they are more remote
and more mysterious, less under the rigid inspection of
our eyes and instruments. Passionately Browne pleads,
as if pointing to his cases of butterflies, his *hortus siccus*,
his anatomical preparations, and all the apparatus of
his study in Norwich, for a patient and unbiassed
examination of little physical things, for a recognition

of their individual value, for an honest effort not to
weave fairy-tales about them and perpetuate a gabble
of superstitions, but to praise God in their reality and
in the harmony of their construction. Such words as
the following fell upon the ears of the seventeenth
century with a sense of absolute novelty; they made
an appeal to a new instinct, to mental powers hitherto
unawakened : —

"I hold there is a general beauty in the works of God,
and therefore no deformity in any kind or species of creature
whatsoever. I cannot tell by what logic we call a toad, a
bear, or an elephant ugly; they being created in those outward shapes and figures which best express the actions of
their inward forms, and having past that general visitation
of God, who saw that all that He had made was good, that
is, conformable to His will, which abhors deformity, and is
the rule of order and beauty. There is no deformity but in
monstrosity; wherein, notwithstanding, there is a kind of
beauty, Nature so ingeniously contriving the irregular parts as
they become sometimes more remarkable than the principal
fabric. To speak yet more narrowly, there was never anything
ugly or misshapen but the Chaos ; wherein, notwithstanding,
to speak strictly, there was no deformity, because no form ;
nor was it yet impregnated by the voice of God. Now Nature
is not at variance with Art, nor Art with Nature, they being
both servants of His Providence. Art is the perfection of
Nature. Were the world now as it was the sixth day, there
were yet a Chaos. Nature hath made one world and Art
another. In brief, all things are artificial; for Nature is
the Art of God."

We must remind ourselves again of Browne's phrase,
that every man's own reason is his best Œdipus. The
Sphinx which puts the questions is Nature, and while
she supplies problems to be solved, it is for Œdipus
to verify the solutions. We do not find our *medicus*

troubled about large views of scientific philosophy.
With much that is curiously in common with Descartes — of whom, however, he never once makes
mention in any portion of his writings — he differs
radically from him in the breadth of his vision. Both
of these remarkable men seem to have held, simul-
taneously, views with regard to the conditions of
science which were entirely new, and which appear to
us singularly exact and just. But while Descartes
pushed his deductive system beyond the limits of
prudence, and dared to revolutionise physics and
mathematics, Browne, a more timid philosopher if a
more original and charming writer, shrank from the
reduction of the universal essence of things to a
theory. It is a vain, but a tempting speculation to
wonder what kind of an influence Browne would have
exercised if — instead of living (as it would seem) side
by side with Descartes, yet ignorant of his existence —
Browne had been born a generation later, and sub-
jected to the full tide of Cartesian ideas. We might
have possessed a more powerful philosopher, but,
almost certainly, a less fascinating artist.

For, before we have reached the middle of *Religio
Medici*, we have discovered that it is an artist
with whom we have to deal, and not a philosopher.
There seemed a chance, as the argument opened, that
we should find here the apology of a new mind. But
we are soon persuaded that our *medicus* belongs to
the class of those who are, as Huxley put it, the
mirrors of their age, not to the class of those who
express the thoughts which, in two or three centuries,
will be the thoughts of everybody. Browne is not,
we discover, an inaugurator of this species. He stands,

in virtue of the fine and reasonable qualities of his
intellect, a little ahead of his contemporaries, but not
much, and he never advances so far as to lose sight of
them. In short, he is not so eminent as a thinker as
he is as a writer; and we resign ourselves to the
immense pleasure of hearing the average ideas of intelligent persons in the early part of the seventeenth
century placed before us in the best possible way. If
we want something quite new, something that was
to speed the world violently forward along its intellectual track, then we must turn to Spinoza or Descartes, and the men who contributed to the movement
of thought. In Browne thought is moderately static,
but it is rendered in enchanting forms, and in a studied
harmony of language.

These reflections become necessary to our enjoyment of *Religio Medici*, when the author starts on a
consideration of his personal attitude in face of what
he had somewhat earlier called "the meanders and
labyrinths of providence." He is eager to deal with
the subject of miracles, on which he expatiates at
length. He admits the existence of the miraculous
with a lightheartedness that is perhaps a little
deceptive. Is he so confident as he declares himself
to be ? His position is that the age of wonder never
passes; that all violent acts of disturbance are equally
easy to God, if to perform them is His will; that the
physical world is full of miracles; and that we must
beware lest we narrowly confine the power of God.
The result of these concessions is that Browne accepts,
and with an alacrity which might even alarm the
clergy whose criticism he deprecates, everything that
is supernatural in religious tradition and anecdote. At

the shrine of the piety of his day, he sacrifices all the results of analytical demonstration and rational research. We are not entirely consoled by the statement that pious frauds, performed with bits of holy wood, or with consecrated swords and roses, are contemptible, because we see more of the Protestant in this than of the philosopher.

We then reach the burning question of witches, where it is melancholy to find that our physician had advanced no whit ahead of his fierce and ignorant contemporaries. He does not question the existence, nor the malign action, of evil spirits. "I have ever believed, and do now know, that there are witches." Indeed, he loses for once all his moderation and his amenity, and calls those who do not share his belief "atheists," a word which, in the early seventeenth century, bore a moral and social, no less than a theological stigma. The expression "do now know" reads like an interpolation, and suggests that Browne had, perhaps since he came to Norwich, been personally engaged in one of those hideous witch-trials which were the disgrace of the age. Or, as the book was written in 1635, this may very likely be a reference to the condemnation of the unhappy women at the Lancashire assizes early in that year, which attracted immense popular interest. We shall have, in a later chapter, to record the most melancholy incident of Browne's career, the part he took, in 1664, in the judicial murder of Rose Cullender and Amy Duny. Here, in *Religio Medici*, he confesses to an implicit faith in prodigies, in prognostics, in short in a whole world of superstition with regard to which it is impossible to say that he was in any sense ahead of his time.

It is pleasant to turn from this painful matter to a field of innocent speculation, where Browne's graceful and melodious style has free course. He declares his confident belief in the neo-Platonic theory of an undivided and common spirit animating the whole world. " Man is a microcosm, partaking of the nature of all created essences," in which in fact you may see the universe reflected, as in a very small pool you can discern at night the vault of heaven and all the infinitude of stars. He is full of the doctrines of Paracelsus, a philosopher who appears at this time, and not at this time only, to have exercised a commanding influence over Browne's intelligence. There were many reasons why the career and opinions of the Swiss visionary should fascinate our Norwich doctor. Paracelsus, who had now been dead for just a hundred years, was a physician who took the widest possible view of the relationship of man to the universe, and whose contributions to the actual practice of medicine had been equally bold and incessant. Sluggishness and timidity, indeed, had never been charged against Paracelsus, whose ceaseless activity led many in his own time, and in the succeeding century, to accuse him of being a fraudulent quack. What Paracelsus really was — beyond being an intellectual creature of the fieriest energy — the world has not yet decided. To his disciple, it is quite plain, he appeared an ideal of what the experimental scientific physician should be, a model of sanity and good works, and a promoter of that vague neo-Platonism which was so dear to the nature of Thomas Browne.

In *Religio Medici*, however, Browne rejects the Montpellier theory of vitalism, by virtue of which the soul

was held to be an organic part of the fabric of man, a
fluid film, perhaps faintly luminous, pervading the
human structure, in the removal of which consisted
the fact of death. Browne had sought for evidences
of the presence of this visible instrument of life in a
series of careful anatomical operations, and he had become convinced that it does not exist. He found that
there is no organ in the whole fabric of man which it
is permissible to suppose the seat of this essential soul.
He had come to the conclusion that, even in the brain,
"which we term the seat of reason, there is not anything of moment more than I can discover in the crany
of a beast, and this is a sensible and no inconsiderable
argument of the inorganity of the soul." Yet on this
subject we may be led to believe that Browne's mind
was not absolutely made up, since in another place he
uses the vitalist formula with approval, and expresses
the opinion that "the immortal spirit and incorrupti-
ble substance of my soul" may sleep awhile "within
this house of flesh." He uses the picturesque but un-
convincing illustration of the metamorphosis of silk-
worms, the moth, like the soul, having existed in
embryo in the body of the chrysalis.

In common with so many of his more imaginative
contemporaries, Browne is lifted to a strange exaltation
by the consideration of mortality. He has observed in
other medical men that the habit of cutting up dead
bodies, or, as he puts it, the "continual raking into the
bowels of the deceased," has led to an insensibility in
the presence of death. The imagination becomes easily
quenched by familiarity. He tells us that he is glad
to say that no such callousness has ever affected himself. The daily habit of a doctor's life has not stupefied

his sensibility in these matters, nor the "continual sight of anatomies, skeletons, or cadaverous relics, like vespilloes or grave-makers," made him stupid. Oddly enough, he attributes something of his freshness of mind in face of the mysteries of mortality to his study of the Philosopher's Stone, which, he declares, "hath taught me a great deal of divinity." We find ourselves wandering, under the charge of this urbane and learned guide, through a strange twilight of mingled intelligence and credulity.

On the subject of the resurrection of the body, which very naturally rises out of the consideration of its tendency to decay, Browne makes a kind of confession which is in his best manner. We must quote but a fragment of its long-drawn music : —

"I believe that our estranged and divided ashes shall unite again ; that our separated dust, after so many pilgrimages and transformations into the parts of minerals, plants, animals, elements, shall at the Voice of God return into their primitive shapes, and join again to make up their primary and predestinate forms. As at the Creation there was a separation of that confused mass into its species, so at the destruction thereof there shall be a separation into its distinct individuals. . . . Let us speak naturally and like philosophers. The forms of alterable bodies in these sensible corruptions perish not ; nor, as we imagine, wholly quit their mansions, but retire and contract themselves into their secret and unaccessible parts, where they may best protect themselves from the action of their antagonist. A plant or vegetable consumed to ashes to a contemplative and school-philosopher seems utterly destroyed, and the form to have taken his leave for ever. But to a sensible artist the forms are not perished, but withdrawn into their incombustible part, where they lie secure from the action of that devouring element. This is made good by experience, which can from the ashes of a plant revive the plant, and from its cinders recall it unto its stalk and leaves again. What the art of man can do in these inferior pieces, what blasphemy is it to affirm the finger of God cannot do in these more perfect and sensible structures? This is that mystical philosophy, from whence no true scholar becomes an atheist, but from the visible effects of nature grows up a real divine, and beholds not in a dream, as Ezekiel, but in an ocular and visible object, the types of his resurrection."

This notion of the revival in life and beauty of a flower which had been reduced to ashes frequently recurs in the circle of Browne's friends. In 1648, Dr. Henry Power repeatedly entreated Browne to carry out the experiment and perform " the reindividualling of an incinerated plant," importuning the physician so repeatedly that Power had to apologise at last for his insistence. It was felt that such an act of re-creation, reversing the natural order of decay, would throw a wonderful light upon the mystery of the resurrection. Various Continental chemists had vaguely described it as possible, but it was felt by his English friends that Browne, and Browne alone, was fitted to unravel so noble and admirable a secret. But Browne seems to have been coy in undertaking the experiment, and to have held the enthusiasm of his disciples in restraint. This was a typical instance of the way in which his imaginative instinct and his rapid flights of rhetoric carried him into an atmosphere which his excellent common sense declined to breathe.

In the desultory course of *Religio Medici,* our physician now gives us his ideas about hell and eternal punishment. He is full of surprises, and on this subject, which we should have expected him to touch rather timidly, he is instinct with courage and fine feeling. " I thank God," he cries, "and with joy I mention it, I was never afraid of Hell, nor never grew pale at the description of that place." We have not begun to know Thomas Browne if we have not yet discovered him to be an optimist, one for whom Providence had painted the whole wide world in rose-colour. To such a temperament as his, hell could offer no terrors, because it could never concentrate his attention. He was delighted with life, with all its gentle pleasures and multiform excitements, and it was not possible for him to see anything at the end of life, far away and closing the vista, except a vision of a heaven which should be like life, only still more brilliantly illuminated. Into such a conception of existence as the sunny, optimist character of Browne had instinctively formed there was no place for the idea of hell; " that terrible term has never detained me from sin, nor do I owe any good action to the name thereof." He fancies that others must be like him; he cannot believe that any one can be " scared " into a virtuous disposition; and in the awful justice of God, upon which the sour theology of the age loved to dilate in horror, Browne can see nothing but "an abyss and mass of mercies."

In his own existence of thirty years he tells us that everything has turned out for his happiness and profit. Even what others consider "crosses, afflictions, judgments, misfortunes," when they have come his way, have presently shown themselves to be blessings in disguise. No wonder that Browne was prepared to believe in good fortune and a lucky star, for he seems to have been one of those few men who have passed through life in an unbroken state of felicity. But in thus expressing his adoring debt of gratitude to God, Browne unconsciously reveals once more his temperament. There are, no doubt, persons who are "lucky" and others who are unlucky. But more than half the secret of happiness lies locked up in our own bosoms, and fate has to strike heavily indeed before it breaks down the cheerfulness of a spirit that is instinctively cheerful. In this Browne is almost alone among philosophers, who are not, on the whole, a happy band. Even Montaigne has his dejected moods, and declares that " le n'avoir point de mal, c'est le plus avoir de bien que l'homme puisse espérer." Browne would not have been content with that; he would have lifted his hands with a smile and an *O altitudo!* and would have declared that to live at all was to have secured a wealth beyond rubies.

He speaks of " the humour of my irregular self," and in truth we learn to deliver ourselves up to it. We hardly know how to take him, when, close upon his cheerful disquisitions upon hell, we find him discoursing upon the pity of sectarianism. Browne is all for making the distinctions between Christians disappear. A few differences of opinion ought not to be allowed to break up the Church of God. The phrase " little flock," as used for those who are in the right way of faith, doth not comfort but deject his devotion. There was no Calvinistic separatism about Browne; with the German poet of a later age, he cried, " Seid umschlungen, Millionen," and in fancy cast his arms around a vast and homogeneous Church of all the world. He took a lenient view of others' faults of doctrine, being, it is perhaps not uncharitable to say, somewhat vague and ductile in his own convictions. He wished to believe what the majority of Christians believed; nay, he insisted upon doing so. But the details of dogma did not interest him, and he dealt in generalities because his mind was not equipped for theological disputation. If Browne was a heretic, as some declared, there certainly never lived a heretic more anxious to be orthodox or less partial to his own errors.

But it is with a definition of faith, and with a visible determination to be subdued to it, that the main argument of *Religio Medici* closes. When we come to think what it is that the whole treatise has amounted to, we perceive that it has been both evasive and para-doxical. Evasive, because the real object of the author — apart from his very manifest artistic object, to write a beautiful book — has been to present an apology for carrying on a secular calling. That is what Browne, a doctor in general country practice, has wanted to do, but he has chosen to do it evasively, by discussing a great number of semi-theological points, many of which, it is obvious, really interest him very little. And paradoxically, because the whole treatise, in its golden haziness, like a meadow flooded with slanting light at sunset, gives us an idea that the author really loved paradox for its own sake, and that his extraordinary leaps and somersaults are made out of solemn freakish-ness, to amuse his own gay and gentle nature, and to dazzle the ingenuous reader a little. We must never forget that *Religio Medici* was written " for my private exercise and satisfaction." It had no purpose of education or edification; it was a sort of diary of the author's soul, a note-book into which he jotted his spiritual symptoms.

Somebody seems to have reminded him that he had

dealt exclusively with faith, and that he ought to say something about charity. Accordingly, he added a sort of appendix, the second part of *Religio Medici*, in which he jots down a number of reflections which had escaped his memory or had occurred to him later. The beauty of his singular style is nowhere in his writings more apparent than here. He is eloquent, of course, about charity, a quality which came to him easily, for, as he tells us, he had borrowed a merciful disposition and a humane inclination from his parents, of whom we can but regret that he has told us so little. He finds in himself a tendency to like every individual person he meets. If he hates anything it is that enemy of reason and virtue, the Multitude, a mass of beings, each one of whom means well, but who collect into one body of stupidity and error. This gives Browne a welcome occasion for a defence of the dignity of individual man, from which he returns to assure us of his own benevolence. We had no doubt of it, but we cannot help beginning to perceive that his charity is founded not so much on reason as on hope and inclination and on an easy-going temper.

The close of the second part of *Religio Medici* is pure autobiography, and Browne gossips in it as no man except Montaigne had ever gossiped before. He is, in English, the earliest prose-writer who dwells with a delicate complacency upon his own natural instincts and the distinguishing features of his temperament. When an author of Browne's exquisite skill takes us into his confidence, and tells us the little secrets of his soul, it would be worse than useless to paraphrase what he says; we are forced to quote his very words. When he talks in such harmonies as those which

follow, our island seems full of sweet airs. He tells us
that he is naturally amorous of all that is beautiful : —

"I can look a whole day with delight upon a handsome
picture, though it be but of an horse. It is my temper, and
I like it the better, to affect all harmony; and sure there is
music even in the beauty, and the silent note which Cupid
strikes, far sweeter than the sound of an instrument. For
there is a music wherever there is a harmony, order, or proportion; and thus far we may maintain the music of the
spheres; for those well-ordered motions, and regular paces,
though they give no sound unto the ear, yet to the understanding they strike a note most full of harmony. Whosoever
is harmonically composed delights in harmony; which makes
me much distrust the symmetry of those heads which declaim
against all church music. For myself, not only from my
obedience, but my particular genius, I do embrace it : for even
that vulgar and tavern-music, which makes one man merry,
another mad, strikes in me a deep fit of devotion and a profound contemplation of the First Composer. There is something in it of divinity more than the ear discovers. It is an
hieroglyphical and shadowed lesson of the whole world, and
creatures of God. Such a melody to the ear, as the whole
world, well understood, would afford the understanding. In
brief, it is a sensible fit of that harmony which intellectually
sounds in the ears of God."

Had not Dryden been reading this admirable passage
when he began his *Song for St. Cecilia's Day*?

"From harmony, from heavenly harmony,
    This universal frame began ";

and the whole ode seems to be but an expansion of
Browne's Platonic fancy. Here, as in so many cases,
the style of our physician is melted into the pure
frenzy of beauty, which gives it its form and texture,
as though in defiance of the author's grave intention.

Like some Italian of the Renaissance, born two hundred years earlier, Browne seems intoxicated with the new-born sense of loveliness, and his style totters with ecstasy. We see his writing, too, in such passages of *Religio Medici* as this, in the comparative freshness of its early felicity, before the Latinisms had overwhelmed him. Here we have nothing to excuse, nothing to smile at or regret; all is sensuous and simple.

A great part of the charm which successive generations of readers have found in *Religio Medici* resides in the confidence with which the writer speaks of himself, especially towards the close of the Second Part. The man's human sympathy, and his delicate comprehension of the limits of those distinctions which should make us the more interested in one another, and, as a fact, are so apt to lead to suspicion and dissension — these are the qualities, rare at all times and almost unique in the seventeenth century, which make this book stand alone among its fellows. Just as a bright and genial companion, talking sympathetically about himself, has the power to persuade his listener that their instincts and aspirations are identical, so all manner of different persons have seen their own characters reflected in Thomas Browne's flattering mirror. It is difficult, for instance, to think of a man of reflective temper less like Browne than S. T. Coleridge was, yet Coleridge seems to have told Wordsworth that he had never read a book in which he found evidence of so close a similarity to his own make of mind as he found in *Religio Medici*. Every one recognises, or believes that he recognises, the best parts of his moral and intellectual nature in Browne's affectionate confidences, and the amenity of the writer is so extreme that the reader easily overlooks the fact that there may be points of unlikeness which are no less important in the general sum of character.

It is proper that we should now turn to the history of this remarkable book, which offers some episodes of unique interest. We have seen that the treatise was written in 1635 or 1636, in company with "some others of affinity thereto," at leisurable hours, and for the author's private exercise and satisfaction. Browne says plainly that his object was not publication, a fact which he considers is made obvious by the familiar and personal character of many of the expressions. It "was penned in such a place," namely, Shipden Hall, at Halifax, where from the first setting of pen unto paper, Browne "had not the assistance of any good book whereby to promote my invention or relieve my memory." He considered, therefore, or modestly affected to consider, that it was not a treatise which could. endure the criticism of the learned, who were inclined in those days to investigate small points of deficient erudition while leaving the whole course of. the argument unexamined. The upshot of the affair was that Browne was pleased with the result of his lucubrations, and could not help showing it to his friends, who asked to be allowed to transcribe so original and so beautiful a little book.

In 1642 one of these manuscript transcripts fell into the hands of a London publisher, Andrew Crooke, who, without obtaining the author's permission, brought it out in the form of a small octavo. This, the first edition of *Religio Medici*, is a very curious little volume. It has no title-page, but there is an engraved frontispiece, designed and cut by William Marshall, the leading book-illustrator of that day. This fantastic plate, which has become familiar to the readers of Browne, represents a man who has leaped, or been hurled, from a rock, but who is caught in mid-air before he reaches the sea beneath him, by a hand from the sky. Help comes to him from heaven: *a cœlo salus.* There is another edition of the text, published in the same way and in the same year, but with closer type, which is no less curious and rare. These pirated editions are entirely anonymous, and possess no prefatory matter of any kind. It is the bare text of *Religio Medici,* put forth without revision. Browne calls these early editions "broken and imperfect" copies, founded upon a text, which by frequent transcription had "still run forward in corruption"; and he accuses them of "the addition of some things, omission of others, and transposition of many." He speaks of them as so "disguised" that the author would be justified if he refused to acknowledge them as his.

In all this, Browne speaks with the exaggeration of an author who has been taken at a disadvantage by a crafty publisher. As he turned the pages of the piracy he would observe little misprints and tiresome divergences from what he had written, which would be enough to disturb his equanimity and yet are not enough to deserve the language which he uses about them. The late Dr. Greenhill collated the piracies with the text issued by Browne himself in 1643, and he found the errors to be singularly few and of no great importance. In any case, the editions of 1642 attracted many readers and were more and more widely discussed. The book might, however, have been slow in attracting general attention, if it had not been for a happy accident. A copy of it fell into the hands of Edward Sackville, Earl of Dorset, who was acting as commissioner of the king's treasury at Oxford. This accomplished nobleman, whose virtues are celebrated by Clarendon, and of whose "beautiful and graceful and vigorous person" Vandyke has transmitted to us a charming portrait, was so much delighted with *Religio Medici* that he warmly recommended it to his friends, and particularly to Sir Kenelm Digby, in a letter written on the 19th of December 1642.

One of the most ardent and versatile figures of that romantic age, Sir Kenelm Digby, like Thomas Browne, had enjoyed the advantages of a Continental education. He also had devoted himself to scientific investigation, although in a more amateurish spirit than Browne, and with much less of the true modesty of experiment. He had early become famous in connection with a kind of anodyne which he called the Sympathetic Powder; and he said that a religious Carmelite had entrusted this remedy to him as a secret he had learned in Persia. It is said that Bacon interested himself in this powder, the rumour of whose properties led to Digby's being patronised and knighted at the age of twenty, by King James I. Digby fitted out a small fleet in the Mediterranean, after the king's death, and harried the Algerines and the Venetians. Having been a member of the Church of England since his childhood, in 1636 he was reconverted to Rome during a visit to Paris. He then became a pamphleteer on the subject of the choice of a religion; and altogether, in his philosophy and his adventurous imagination, and his plea for liberty of religious opinion, he was not merely an exhilarating contemporary figure, but he had more than a little in common with Browne himself.

Though his ideas were neither exact nor profound, there was that about the stirring character of Sir Kenelm Digby which made him accepted by his contemporaries as an authority both in science and in religion. If a book of the class of *Religio Medici* was published, there were a great many people who would be interested in knowing what Sir Kenelm Digby thought of it. Since 1639, when the House of Commons had ordered him to give an account of the Catholic contribution, he had been looked upon as a leader of the more liberal section of his community, while he was an ardent and outspoken Royalist. Staying in London when the Civil War broke out, Digby was arrested by the Parliament and confined in Winchester House. This imprisonment, however, was a very mild one ; the Catholic philosopher had his own servants, free communication with the world outside, and great respect from his captors. But his native restlessness displayed itself in a feverish mental activity, and Sir Kenelm Digby was now prepared to write a striking pamphlet upon almost any subject.

Although it was already late in the evening when Sir Kenelm Digby received Lord Dorset's letter advising him to read *Religio Medici*, he was so much struck by what his noble friend had written that he sent his servant out immediately to St. Paul's Churchyard to endeavour to buy a copy. The shops were shutting, no doubt, and the messenger delayed his return ; Sir Kenelm Digby meanwhile went to bed. He was not yet asleep, however, when his man came back, having succeeded in buying one of the pirated editions. Sir Kenelm, writing next morning (December 23, 1642) to Lord Dorset, excitedly reports : —

"This good-natured creature [*Religio Medici*] I could easily persuade to be my bedfellow, and to wake with me as long as I had any edge to entertain myself with the delights I sucked from so noble a conversation. And truly, my Lord, I closed not my eyes till I had enriched myself with, or at least exactly surveyed, all the treasures that are lapped up in the folds of those few sheets."

But when he had sunk to sleep at last, having taken, as Browne might himself have said, this merciful dormitive to bedward, intellectual excitement would not suffer Sir Kenelm Digby to rest quiet. In the early morning, almost before it was light, he woke, and then and there — as it appears, in his bed — he began to compose a criticism on the marvellous book which had so greatly amazed his spirits. This critical examination of *Religio Medici*, which formed, when printed, a little volume of one hundred and twenty-four pages, was written almost at a sitting, in a blaze of enthusiasm and excitement.

It does not appear that either Dorset or Digby at this time knew the name of the author whose book had interested them so much. But a little later on, Sir Kenelm seems to have put himself in communication with Andrew Crooke, the publisher, who informed Browne that the famous Catholic philosopher was preparing to print a review of *Religio Medici*. It is almost certain that it was this information which induced Browne to remove the embargo he had placed upon his work, and to supply Crooke with a revised and correct manuscript to print from. Meanwhile, the knight had received back his letter from Lord Dorset,

and had allowed it to be sent to the press.   In a panic
of vexation, on the 3rd of March 1643, Browne wrote
from Norwich to Sir Kenelm Digby, entreating him
to delay the publication of that criticism of which he
had " descended to be the author," until the genuine
text of the original, which Browne said he was now
hastening through the printer's hands, could be referred to.   The demand was a reasonable one, presented
in the most courteous terms, but it reached Winchester
House too late, or else Digby's vanity would not brook
delay, for there appeared at the end of March 1643
a volume of *Observations upon Religio Medici*, " occasionally written " by Sir Kenelm Digby, Knight.   After
the briefest possible further delay, Crooke issued " a
true and full copy of that which was most imperfectly
and surreptitiously printed before under the name of
Religio Medici."   We see that, once having secured the
correct text of this popular book, the publisher was
ready to acknowledge, without a blush, that his previous editions of it had been "imperfect " and even
" surreptitious."   The public, however, had at last
what is known as the first authorised edition, that
of 1643.

The incidents which have just been recorded are not
merely curious and interesting in themselves, but they
mark a condition in which Browne was almost, if not
quite, unique among the English authors of his time.
The absence of accepted critical authority, applied to
literature, was an extreme inconvenience to the writers
of the early seventeenth century.   A critical feeling
was abroad, but it had not yet found any vehicle, nor
was it concentrated on particular publications; there
was no one until the time of Dryden, who was in a

position to create critical values. The result was that
books fell suddenly into complete discredit in consequence of a slight change in the current of popular
taste, and did not recover until modern criticism went
back to dig for them under the dust of two centuries.
If we consider certain admirable publications of the
same decade as *Religio Medici*, if we take, for instance, Milton's *Poems* of 1645, and Herrick's *Hesperides*
of 1648, we find ourselves in the presence of works
which acquired no public valuation in their own time,
which attracted no examination and no movement of
opinion, and which, in consequence, sank immediately
into discredit as soon as the taste of the moment
deviated from that in which they had been composed.
It may be said, without paradox, that the reputation
of Herrick and Milton as lyrical poets did not begin
to exist until modern criticism rediscovered them, and
almost, indeed, created them.

It was Browne's extraordinary good fortune to enjoy
contemporary criticism. He was defended and he was
attacked, but at least he did not sink under that fatal
silence which attended the bulk of the works of his
contemporaries. The *Observations* of Sir Kenelm Digby
gave a definite value to *Religio Medici*. People who
read the latter were pleased to know what were the
conclusions of the Roman Catholic critic, and they
adopted or rejected them as the case might be. Discussion was awakened, and it moved on a definite
basis. The success of Browne's book was marked, and
public curiosity was proved by the issue, so early as
1644, of a revised edition of Digby's *Observations*. Other
censors hurried forward, who agreed neither with
Digby nor with Browne. Their pamphlets, whether

hostile or laudatory, increased the excitement around
the original text, and the Norwich physician found
himself one of the most eminent writers of the day.
Curiosity in his book spread quickly to the continent
of Europe; and already in 1644 two editions were published in Latin, one in Leyden and the other in Paris.

The author of the earliest Latin version, in a letter
addressed five years later to Browne, gives some
curious particulars as to the reception of *Religio
Medici* in Holland and in France. The first publisher
to whom this John Merryweather offered his manuscript
took it to Salmasius, who was the great glory of Leyden,
and now regarded as the literary dictator of Europe.
Salmasius, who knew very little indeed about English
affairs, nevertheless posed as a great defender of the
Stuart crown, and was pleased to be the opponent of
Milton, and consulted about English politics. He kept
the Latin *Religio Medici* by him for three months, and
then told the translator that "it contained many
things well said, but also many exorbitant conceptions
in religion," and that it would "probably find but
frowning entertainment." The translator, however,
persisted until he discovered a Leyden printer willing
to undertake it.

From Leyden, copies of Merryweather's translation
were sent to all parts of western Europe, and they
seem to have been welcomed everywhere. But the
most gratifying reception which they met with was in
Paris, where the book arrived in October 1644. Of
the fate of the book among the French we have very
interesting evidence scattered through the sparkling,
easy, and sarcastic letters which Guy Patin addressed to
his friends. This eminent physician was at that time

one of the leaders of European opinion. A man of the highest scientific attainments, dean of the faculty of medicine in Paris, and king's lecturer at the Collège de France, Guy Patin had opportunities of extending the reputation of a new book such as were shared by few. He was orthodox, yet liberal; a man of advanced ideas, yet untainted by the charge of atheism. An experimental philosopher, a practical physician, a brilliant man of letters, Patin's position was not without a certain likeness to that of the Norwich *medicus*, but it was as central as Browne's was provincial. The earliest of Patin's references to the new English volume occurs in a letter of October 1644 : —

" Un petit livre nouveau intitulé *Religio Medici* fait par un Anglais et traduit en latin par quelque Hollandais. C'est un livre tout gentil et curieux, mais fort délicat et tout mystique ; l'auteur ne manque pas d'esprit ; vous y verrez d'étranges et ravissantes pensées. Il n'y a encore guère de livres de cette sorte. S'il était permis aux savants d'écrire ainsi librement, on nous apprendroit beaucoup de nouveautés . . . la subtilité de l'esprit humain se pourroit découvrir par cette voie."

This is by far the most penetrating contemporary judgment which, so far as we know, was passed on *Religio Medici*. Nothing to approach it, indeed, was said, until Coleridge began to scribble notes on the edges of the reprint of 1802. It was probably owing to the interest awakened by Guy Patin, that although there was another Leyden edition of 1644, this did not suffice for Paris. Merryweather told Browne : —

" When I came to Paris the next year [1645], I found it printed again, in which edition both the Epistles were left out, and a preface by some papist put in their place, in which, making use of, and wresting some passages in your book, he endeavoured to show that nothing but custom and education kept you from their Church."

This Paris reprint created a great stir in France, where some people took the view indicated by the preface, while others were inclined to charge the author with heresy and infidelity. Guy Patin again comes to our help in a delightful letter of April 16, 1645, addressed to the Troyes physician, Belin : —

"On fait ici grand état du livre intitulé *Religio Medici*; cet auteur a de l'esprit. C'est un mélancholique agréable en ses pensées, mais qui, à mon jugement, cherche maître en fait de religion, comme beaucoup d'autres, et peut-être qu'enfin il n'en trouvera aucun. Il faut dire de lui ce que Philippe de Commines a dit du fondateur des Minimes, l'ermite de Calabre, François de Paule, ' Il est encore en vie, il peut aussi bien empirer qu'amender ! ' "

This is very amusing, and we may suspect that the adroit Parisian critic hoped to see Browne come forth in more definite revolt. He was disappointed, if so, but he never lost his interest in *Religio Medici*. When, in 1652, a certain Levin Nicholas Moltke put forth a tedious and pedantic sheet of *Annotations*, Guy Patin flew into a passion at the impertinence of the man, and declared that such good wine as *Religio Medici* needed no presumptuous German bush. As late as 1657 we find Patin true to his enthusiastic admiration of Thomas Browne, " si gentil et éveillé " ; and when Edward Browne was in Paris in 1664, Patin, meeting him in a shop by accident, " saluted me very kindly, asked me many things concerning my father, whom he knew only as author of *Religio Medici*, discoursed with me very lovingly, and told me he would write to my father." Thomas Browne was eager to hear more

about his first kind critic, and Edward, who attended
Patin's physic lectures, tells him that Patin "is very
old, yet very pleasant in his discourse and hearty; he
is much followed [in Paris], is a Galenist, and doth
often laugh at the chymists"; after the lectures, "he
answers all doubts and questions proposed." In September 1665, further courtesies having passed, we find
Browne telling his son to "present my services and
thanks unto Dr. Patin," who lived on until 1672, dying
full of honours and fame. The whole episode of his
relations with Browne is one of great interest, the
more as it was unparalleled at that time in the literary
history of England and France.

The spread of Browne's fame over the continent
of Europe was rapid. As early as 1649, a foreign
correspondent was able to assure him that "a good
part of Christendom" was now familiar with his
character and work. For a century his name continues to recur in the heavy German discussions about
atheism and superstition, some writers claiming that
Browne was a freethinker, others defending his orthodoxy. Buddæus of Jena, drawing up a list of English
atheists, put Sir Thomas Browne's name into it, along
with those of Lord Herbert of Cherbury, Hobbes, and
Toland; while Tobias Wagner, a pillar of the German
Church in his day, declared that *Religio Medici* could
scarcely be read without danger of infection. All this
was lumbering and ill-informed criticism, but it proves
that the Norwich physician had achieved a foreign
reputation denied to the rest of his contemporaries.
When, in 1652, Levin Nicholas Moltke published his
Annotations, he said that he had been first led to
the perusal of *Religio Medici* by its universal fame in

England, France, Italy, Holland, and Germany; and he
declared that at the time he wrote all those countries
were ringing with the applause of Browne. Nor was
this vogue confined to the Latin version, for before
Browne died, his book had appeared in French,
German, Dutch, and Italian translations.

To return to England, and to the most important of
all the native criticisms of Browne, a study of Sir
Kenelm Digby's *Observations* of 1643 shows that what
"thoroughly touched the little needle" of the knight's
soul was the happy temper of spiritual liberty which
breathed from every page of *Religio Medici*. Digby,
who had been writing a treatise on the immortality of
the soul, was attracted by the Platonism of Browne,
with which he found himself in ardent sympathy. But
he thought the physician a little too much bound down
to earth by his habits of physical experiment, and he
would fain have found his conceptions of eternity more
transcendental. Yet "his wishes and aims, and what
he pointeth at, speak him owner of a noble and a
generous heart." On one point, Sir Kenelm Digby
rises superior to Browne, whom he challenges, with
great courage, for "knowing that there are witches."
It was highly dangerous in those days to deny the
existence of such malevolent powers. Digby does not
go so far. "I only reserve my assent," he says, "till I
meet with stronger motives to carry it. And I confess
I doubt much of the efficacy of those magical rules he
speaketh of, as also of the finding out of mysteries by
the courteous revelation of spirits."

Many of Sir Kenelm's thrusts with the rapier are
highly effective. When he says that we cannot err in
taking the author of *Religio Medici* for "a very fine

ingenious gentleman, but how deep a scholar" he will
not presume to say, he insists on what modern criticism
must constantly repeat, that it is the art, the style,
the human charm of Browne that matter, and not his
boasted learning. For his metaphysical arguments,
Digby depends upon Thomas White, the Albius of
Roman controversy, who was presently to push his
own speculations into dangerous fields. It is odd that
he reproves the personal note in Brown's treatise,
and those confidences about himself, and his tasks
and habits, which we enjoy so much. To Digby it
seemed that these could "not much conduce to any
man's betterment"; and he urged Browne to omit
them from his treatises of philosophy, reserving them
for that "notable romance of his own story and life"
which he doubted not that Browne might "profitably
compose." The *Observations*, however, although occasionally carping, are full of appreciative comment, and
Sir Kenelm's summing-up of "our physician," as he
calls Browne, is worth quoting: —

"Truly I must needs pay him as a due the acknowledging
his pious discourses to be excellent and pathetical ones, containing worthy motives, to incite one to virtue and to deter
one from vice. . . . Assuredly he is owner of a solid head,
and of a strong, generous heart. Where he employeth his
thoughts upon such things as resort to no higher or more
abstruse principles than such as occur in ordinary conversation with the world, or in the common track of study and
learning, I know no man would say better. But when he
meeteth with such difficulties as concerning the resurrection
of the body, . . . I do not at all wonder he should tread a
little away and go astray in the dark, for I conceive his course
of life hath not permitted him to allow much time unto the
unwinding of such entangled and abstracted subtilties. But,

if it had, I believe his natural parts are such as he might have kept the chair from most men I know, for even where he roveth widest, . . . most assuredly his wit and sharpness is of the finest standard."

Browne was, however, to meet with something other than unstinted praise. Even he was to be the victim of a fierce reviewer. The eccentric poetaster Edward Benlowes, a Catholic who had just turned Protestant and who yearned to show his zeal for Anglican doctrine, urged Alexander Ross, an active Scottish pamphleteer of the age, familiar now to readers of *Hudibras*, to confute the errors of *Religio Medici.* Other friends entreated that Kenelm Digby should be castigated at the same time, and accordingly, in 1645, Ross published *Medicus Medicatus: or the Physician's Religion cur'd by a lenitive or gentle potion.* This was pronounced by John Downham and other rigid Puritans to be a "learned, sound, and solid" contribution to philosophy, and Dr. Johnson writes too hastily when he says that the *Medicus Medicatus* was "universally neglected." There are always several people who are particularly pleased to see a successful writer attacked, and Ross enjoyed a ripple of reaction. That Browne, made too sensitive perhaps by all the flattery of his book, was seriously annoyed seems to be shown by the fact that as late as 1647 his disciples, such as Henry Bates, were still consoling him with assurances, which indeed were true enough, that all Ross had done was "but a foil to set off and illustrate" Browne's "gallant thoughts."

The *Medicus Medicatus*, nevertheless, is clever, and it is a type of the objections which a certain class of mind will always bring against Browne's writings.

Ross calls him sharply to account for his sentimentality, his rhetoric, his looseness of logical sequence. He treats him as a smart schoolmaster treats an absent-minded little boy. There is something very ludicrous in the mode he adopts, for he quotes long passages from *Religio Medici* in order that he may refute them; and we have the illusion that Browne stands there, talking in his dreamy way, only to get a sudden rap over the knuckles from the ferule of the pedagogue. Ross is indignant at Browne's vague tenderness to the Catholics, and is suspicious of his orthodoxy generally. His thrusts are often shrewd enough, and would be telling, if we could only persuade ourselves to look at the visionary, beautiful treatise in this prosaic way. Even Ross submits at last to the exquisite magic of the book, for, after having been as rude to it as possible, he suddenly acknowledges that "there is much worth and good language in it." But this late concession can have done little to soothe the feelings of the ruffled physician of Norwich.

It will be seen by a comparison of all these specimens of contemporary criticism, that the religious aspect of the book offered a difficulty to all readers. What was the author's exact relation to the faith of his time? To this question there was no positive reply, and people accepted or did not accept Browne's eager protestation of his own orthodoxy. We may believe that he was not quite logical himself, and that he was, as we have said, a bewitching artist rather than a penetrative and original thinker. It is amusing to note that Coleridge, when he was reading the earlier sections of *Religio Medici*, came to the con-

clusion that " had Sir T. B. lived nowadays, he would
probably have been a very ingenious and bold infidel."
At other times, Coleridge gives Browne credit for
unshaken faith built upon a humble confidence in
revelation. Perhaps some light on this paradox may
be given by a reference to the vicissitudes of belief in
the conscience of another and a far greater philosopher
of Browne's own age.

We may observe, then, that the attitude of Browne
to religion and science is almost exactly that which
Pascal adopted, with a more lucid definition, in the
Préface du Traité du Vide, published four years later
than *Religio Medici.*   Both the French and the
English philosopher alike held, at that time, that
the two realms are entirely distinct.   In theology all
depends upon authority and tradition, all has been
long ago settled for us for ever.   In science, authority
does not exist in itself, but has to be constantly augmented and verified by the process of experiment.
The one is stationary, the other incessantly in development.   But while Browne, like Pascal, before 1647,
believed in progress and evolution, he believed in
them only in relation to physical knowledge, which
the patient labour of man is for ever making more
full and more exact.   Neither the one nor the other
allowed science to interfere in the slightest degree with
the domain of faith or with the dogmatism of moral
ideas.   Both of them looked upon the generations of
humanity as a single man, whose conduct in the course
of the centuries was guided by one set of stationary
injunctions, beyond and above his powers of discussion, but whose knowledge of physical facts was
continually extending.   To this class of devout inves-

tigator, sincerely pious, but without a .trace of credulity when his attention is called to the phenomena
of physical nature, many eminent men of science have
belonged. We have but to recollect that Michael
Faraday pursued his magnificent investigations in
electromagnetism with the utmost independence, while
at the same time identifying his faith in humble piety
with that of the straitest sect of the Sandemanians.
He claimed, he said, "an absolute distinction between
religious and ordinary belief."

This compromise sufficed for the author of *Religio
Medici* throughout his long life. But the logic of
Pascal was more profound, and his knowledge of
himself more thorough. After his conversion, the
compromise between science and religion became in-
tolerable to him. He wrote that section of the *Pensées*
which treats, with how severe a disdain, " de la folie
de la science humaine et de la philosophie," and he
repudiated as presumptuous the curiosity which had
led him, in his younger days, to attempt to fathom
the mysteries of physical knowledge. He regarded
all attempts at increasing the stores of human equip-
ment as so many futile acts of encouragement given
to man's " dignity " and " greatness," whereas all
knowledge should begin with the acceptance of the
fact that the spirit of man is utterly mean and small,
and can be lifted by no power whatever, except that
of a humble resignation to the will of God. The easy
optimism of Browne was never troubled with these
ascetic scruples. He was much less rigorous a logician
than Pascal, and, besides, he started from different pre-
misses. He pursued his useful and entertaining course
quite indifferent to and unconscious of the agonies and

exultancies which were sapping the vital forces of his great contemporary at Port-Royal. At the moment when Pascal died, worn out by the ecstasy of his faith, "the world forgetting, by the world forgot," Browne was prosperously collecting bird's eggs and medals on week-days, and attending divine worship at St. Peter's church in Norwich upon Sundays. No two careers could have diverged more strangely, yet it is worth remembering that there had been a time, some twenty years before, when the attitude of the two philosophers had been practically identical.

CHAPTER III

THE *VULGAR ERRORS*

BETWEEN the year 1636, when he finished *Religio Medici*, and 1646, when he published in folio his massive *Pseudodoxia Epidemica*, we cannot trace any literary work in which Browne was certainly engaged, other than jotting down and arranging the notes which were to form his " inquiries into very many received tenets and commonly presumed truths, which examined prove but Vulgar and Common Errors." A great sensation had been produced in the course of the previous generation by the publication of two books by the French physician Dr. Laurent Joubert, entitled *Paradoxa Medica* and *De Vulgi Erroribus*. The vogue of these works had been extraordinary, and when Browne was at Montpellier, they still preserved their celebrity. I cannot help thinking that the names of these famous volumes, and something of their scope, unconsciously affected the Norwich physician in the choice of titles for his great treatise, although he is careful to say that he " reaped no advantage " from the study of Joubert, and that he found *De Vulgi Erroribus* " answering scarce at all to the promise of the inscription." Joubert exposed mistakes which empirical doctors were in the habit of making in the treatment of disease, but that was not Browne's purpose in any degree.

Our *medicus* is very anxious that we should give
him credit for the novelty of his design, and we
have to admit that the *Vulgar Errors* (as *Pseudodoxia
Epidemica* is usually and conveniently styled) was a
work of considerable originality. It is plain that the
form it now takes was the result of accident, not of
forethought. The book was composed "by snatches
of time"; Browne quaintly remarking that such a
work as this is not to be "performed upon one leg."
It could not be written rhetorically, as a *tour de force*,
nor, as so much of the so-called rational philosophy of
the preceding age had been written, in the study,
with Philemon Holland's translation of Pliny open at a
desk, and somebody's comment on Dioscorides spread
out upon the floor. It had to be the result of open-
air observation and personal experiment. Browne
had great difficulties in his pursuit of knowledge; as a
physician of steadily growing popularity his door was
never quiet nor his leisure unmolested. In the midst
of a delicate observation, he was liable to be called
away to the bed-side of a patient. But he must have
had a perfect system of note-books, to harmonise with
his insatiable curiosity, and the arrangement of his
scattered material is masterly. His first intention was
to write his book in Latin; but he was happily persuaded that he owed "in the first place this service to
our country," and secondly that such a work was
addressed primarily to the county magnates, to our
own "ingenuous gentry," and that they were beginning to have a difficulty in reading Latin at sight.
Hence, by great good fortune, Browne deigned to
write in English.

He dismissed his bulky folio to the public, not

without a shiver of apprehension. He deprecated the
frown of theology. But he knew by experience that
people love to preserve their mistakes, and are often
heartily vexed to be set right. He was not quite sure.
of the countenance of his brothers in physic, who
might not be pleased at so wholesale a discomfiture
of the errors of mankind. But Browne trusted to the
scythe of time and to the hopeful dominion of truth,
and believed that he would ultimately be regarded
as a public benefactor. It is necessary to remind ourselves that his great object was to enforce experimental
and exact knowledge, to excite the eye and fix it upon
material objects. As a naturalist and a physician,
Browne saw the great error of the age to be an obse-
quious acceptance of traditional accounts of things
which were, really, under our own eyes day after day.
Let us pay less humble a service, he says in effect, to
the much-vaunted ancients. Albertus Magnus had declared that if you hang up a dead kingfisher by the
bill it will " show in what quarter the wind is by an
occult and secret propriety, converting the breast to
that point of the horizon from whence the wind doth
blow." Very well; but on Yare and on Wensum, rivers
of Norfolk, there are plenty of kingfishers. Shoot one
and hang it up, and see for yourself whether it does
show in what quarter the wind is.

Browne's just complaint against the conventional
science of his day was that it turned its back on nature
in a slavish appeal to tradition. It did not trust to
clinical experiment; it repeated for the thousandth
time the formulas of Galen and Hippocrates. It did
not look carefully at animals and plants, it merely
quoted reverently what the disciples of Aristotle had

said. It took for granted, as Browne excellently
remarks, that "intellectual acquisition is but reminis-
cential evocation, and new impressions but the
colouring of old stamps which stood pale in the soul
before." This latter phrase exactly expresses what it
was that Browne had to combat in his more intelligent
readers. They had a dim recollection that it was
understood that the elephant has no joints, and that,
as it cannot lie down, it sleeps erect against a tree.
They looked into their old authorities, and found that
Diodorus Siculus had said this, and that Strabo had
confirmed it. That was enough for them; they had
coloured the old pale stamp in their souls, and this
they thought to be a sufficient pursuit of knowledge
as to the articulation of pachyderms. But Browne
wished to show them that "an old and grey-headed
error" like this is not to be verified and made gospel
of by a reference to what ancient Greek naturalists
may have reported, but should be tested anew by living
facts. He reminds his contemporaries that "not many
years past, we had the advantage in England of an
elephant shown in many parts thereof." Did this
elephant kneel and lie down? To be sure it did, in
the sight of a cloud of witnesses. Why, then, repeat
and repeat the result of a lack of careful observation
on the part of certain ancient authors, merely because
they were ancient?

Browne makes his appearance as the champion of
nature, throwing down the gauntlet to those who
refuse to look "beyond the shell and the obvious
exteriors of things," and who build up theories to
account for that which they have only read about, not
seen or felt. He is in all this the disciple of Bacon, or

would have been, if he had exactly comprehended what
"the lord of Verulam" had designed to teach.   It
was now a quarter of a century since the *Novum
Organum*, and with it a new great light of natural
philosophy, had risen upon the world.   There is no
doubt for us, and there was probably but little doubt
for Browne, that the outline of all future interpretation
of the facts of nature was divined by Bacon in his
celebrated doctrine of the necessity of the systematic
examination of facts.   This was his great contribution
to thought; and if his tremendous *Instauratio*, that
encyclopædia of knowledge, had ever been carried out,
in the third book of it, as Robert Leslie Ellis has
said, "all the phenomena of the universe were to be
stored up in a treasure-house," and were to be the
materials on which the new method of philosophy
was to be employed.   But it seems certain that
Browne was rather dim in his perception of what
Bacon's drift had been, and certainly he shrank from
an enterprise so vast as Bacon had recommended.

We cannot too often remind ourselves in considering
the apparently stationary character of English scientific theory during the thirty years which lay between
the death of Bacon and the rise of the Invisible
Philosophers, that Bacon was at once far ahead of
his time and yet scarcely a stimulating influence.   He
foresaw, he cast forth brilliant intuitions, but he did
not undertake the work which he recommended.   He
speaks of himself, very justly, as of "an image in a
cross-way, that may point out the way, but cannot go
it."   His genius, colossal as it was, was, after all, finite.
In 1591, Bacon, still young and hopeful, told Lord
Burghley that he had tak n all knowledge for his

province, "to purge it of frivolous disputations and
blind experiments." But he was not Briareus or Argus,
and he failed by reason of the enormous scope which
he had set before his mortal hands and eyes. He
wanted to do so much, he saw so much that had to
be done, that he practically did nothing but dream,
and, as he said, point out the way. The scientific men
of the Restoration, who took up at last the gigantic
schemes Bacon had sketched, called him Moses upon
Mount Pisgah, because they perceived that, with all
his clairvoyance, he had never entered the promised
land.

Browne's attitude to this condition must not be
exaggerated. There is no evidence that he had grasped
the plan of Bacon's huge fragments very thoroughly.
He also stood on the slopes of Pisgah, but he aimed at
no tremendous conquests. He had devoted his leisure
to "sober inquiries into the doubtful appertinancies
of arts and receptories of philosophy," but his interest
lay in specific and positive cases, not in wide sweeps
of theoretical reasoning. In the *Vulgar Errors* we find
him a naturalist, rather than a philosopher, just as in
Religio Medici we found him an artist rather than
a theologian. If we chose to be harsh with Browne,
we might find that he himself is not a little victimised
by vulgar errors, tainted with thaumaturgy, tempted
into false and chimerical byways of science, a dabbler
in necromancy, witchcraft, and the philosopher's stone.
On all this posterity does not love to dwell. But we
must take it into consideration when we have to admit
that all his book does is to mark a step on the ladder
of human knowledge, a safe and humdrum step. It
is not a great leap up among the stars like the *Novum*

Organum, and in point of fact there is little profit in trying to compare Browne with Bacon.

But he had certainly learned the one golden rule of the new philosophy, that the examination of facts must always precede generalisation and theory. This is the mainstay of the *Vulgar Errors,* which is a wise book whenever it leans on this principle — an absurd and tottering book whenever it rejects it. Browne's danger — and he seems to have been aware of it — was to fall into fresh error in the very act of exposing error. But he was not very anxious about this, because, as he rather elaborately expresses it, " these weeds," — that is to say, such mistakes as he himself may make — " must lose their alimental sap and wither of themselves," " except they be watered from higher regions and fructifying meteors of knowledge." Perhaps he was thinking of the lamentable errors into which some of the most ardent spirits of the sixteenth century had fallen, such as his own Paracelsus, and that astonishing genius Cardan, who, in his hatred of Aristotle, and in his wild vagaries of speculation, had come to be regarded as the type of the charlatanism of the age, and who yet, in all probability, was at heart a seeker after truth. All this result of confused fancy and disordered erudition was on the borderland of madness; if Browne should by chance fall back across it, his comfort lay in his knowledge that such error is ephemeral.

He had a shocking example of obstinate error in the one direct English predecessor whom he names. Dr. James Primrose, of Hull, like Browne a pupil in the school of Montpellier, had, in 1638, while Browne was at work on his great book, published a treatise, *De Vulgi in Medicina Erroribus,* which was very widely

read.   Unhappily, one of the errors which Dr. Primrose most manfully exposed was Harvey's discovery of
the circulation of the blood.   Primrose was "remarkable for any characteristic rather than that of a candid
spirit in pursuit of truth."   He abounded in obstinate
denial of any new observation, and Willis, in the next
generation, signalled Primrose as one who in the whole
course of his numerous writings "appeals not once
to experiment as a means of investigation."   In his
colleague at Hull, then, Browne had before him an
example of that reaction against the spirit of Bacon
and Harvey which appeared, about 1650, to be fraught
with so many dangers for English science.   It is infinitely to Browne's credit that, with the expectation
of scandal on one side and of error on the other, he
nevertheless summoned up courage "to stand alone
against the strength of opinion and to meet the Goliath
and giant of Authority with contemptible pebbles, and
feeble arguments drawn from the scrip and slender
stock" of his own experiment.

We are too apt to suppose that in exposing vulgar
errors Browne was attacking the errors of the vulgar.
But this was not the case; he did not venture down
into the vast hollows of popular superstition and
ignorance.   The tales he refutes are often so monstrous that we easily fancy that they must have been
those of the unthinking masses; but Browne particularly says that he has not addressed his pen or style
"unto the People, — whom books do not address and
who are in this way incapable of reduction, — but unto
the knowing and leading part of Learning."   Certainly,
a perusal of this volume may give us an astounding
idea of what professors of both universities, clergymen,

doctors, lawyers, and squires believed and perpetuated in the way of superstition while Charles I. was still upon the throne of England. If Browne's light sometimes seems glimmering to us, like that twilight which astronomers say is all that illuminates the planet Jupiter at high noon, what are we to think of the darkness of his contemporaries? The obstinate fault they all indulged was the habit of saying, " Such and such thing is not, because Pliny says it is not." But it moves or grows at your very door; look and see! — " I will not look; Pliny says it is not, therefore it cannot be." It was Browne's aim to awaken an intellectual conscience in the learned men of his time, and to prove to them that they were doing a grave wrong to the race by shutting their eyes against the truth thus obstinately.

He could not destroy supernaturalism by simply contradicting its statements. He had to demonstrate by facts, by an appeal to a present reality, that those statements were not in accordance with fact. His strength, therefore, lay in clinging, through evil report and good report, to what is palpable and visible, since what he was combating was not merely ignorance, it was wilful and bigoted ignorance. False representations in pictures troubled him very much; but in this respect the seventeenth century was inconsistent. It encouraged at once the worst and the best. In the matter of botany, in which Browne took a particular interest, there was the utmost discrepancy between the rude and false drawings of flowers which were commonly distributed, and the woodcuts in Gerard's *Herbal* and in the *Paradisus* of Parkinson, the accuracy of which is scarcely to be impeached by the science of to-day, even when supported by photography. It was a transitional age in which Browne lived, and it culti-vated extremes of ignorance and knowledge which it is difficult for us to appreciate.

It cannot be denied that those chapters of the *Vulgar Errors* which deal with zoology are the most picturesque. Mistakes about minerals and "terreous bodies" no longer excite any emotion, but the cocka-trice and the unicorn are always welcome. This, too, seems to be the section upon which the author has expended most mental energy. It is, however, the barest justice to say that Browne could not have carried out his ingenious and entertaining labours without the aid of a predecessor whom he names, indeed, with consideration, but hardly, we may think, with all that gratitude which his immense services to natural history demanded. Ulisse Aldrovandi, who died at Bologna about the year in which Browne was born, had devoted all his long life and all his con-siderable fortune to the collection and illustration of animal, vegetable, and mineral specimens, and he undertook the crushing task of re-writing, on a vast scale, with plates as accurate as he could make them, and with constant reference to the object before him, the natural history of the world as Pliny had conceived it. He gathered a school of naturalists around him, and set them to work on various sections of the plan; they carried it on long after his death, and, indeed, the enormous book — the first volume of which, treat-ing of birds, had appeared in 1599 — was not completed until 1642, when Browne had already begun to work on the *Vulgar Errors*. Among the naturalists of the early seventeenth century, Aldrovandi was known by

the title of Pontifex Maximus, and he deserved the
distinction. The liberality of his views and his courage
in expressing them led to his being persecuted for
heresy, but Bologna seems to have been proud to protect the high priest of science. In the course of
centuries, the huge illustrated compilation of Aldrovandi, which has neither the picturesqueness of earlier
fabulous zoologies nor the exactitude of later investigation, has come to be treated as waste paper, but it
had a wide effect in clearing away those very popular
errors against which Browne contends.

What is more extraordinary than Browne's lack of
enthusiasm for Aldrovandi, is his almost complete
neglect of Konrad Gesner (1516–65), whose great work,
the *Historia Animalium* (1551–58) he barely refers
to once or twice. Gesner, who is greatly praised by
Cuvier, as practically the founder of modern zoology,
stood in many respects ahead of Browne in the exact
knowledge of facts about animals. The English para-
phrases of Gesner, brought out by the Rev. Edward
Topsell, the *History of Four-Footed Beasts* (1607) and
the *History of Serpents* (1608), had been extremely
popular. These folios, full of amazing pictures, were
the terror and delight of all good Jacobean children ;
and it is certain that Browne must have been familiar
with them.

Browne is happiest when he speaks of what he has
seen himself. For instance, he had been troubled in
mind to know what spermaceti was. The philosophers
had various absurd theories about this substance, but
the one thing they did not do was to examine the
body of a whale. During Browne's early life-time, two
great whales were cast up on the coast of Norfolk, the

first near Wells, the second at Hunstanton. It is a
little doubtful from his language whether, in one of
these instances, he trusted to the report of Sir Hamon
L'Estrange, but in the other case he seems certainly to
have gone down to the shore and cut up the monster
himself. The fishermen called it a "gibbartas," by
which odd name, connected with the word "gib," they
doubtless signified a whale with a hump or bunch on
its back. Browne says it was not a proper "gib-fish,"
but a sperm-whale, doubtless what we should call a
cachalot. The creature had been dead "divers days"
before the anatomist reached it; it stank horridly and
streams of oil and sperm were flowing from its body.
But Browne examined the "magazine of spermaceti,"
and found it "in the head, lying in folds and courses,
in the bigness of goose eggs, encompassed with large
flaky substances as large as a man's head, in form of
honeycombs, very white and full of oil."

The *Vulgar Errors* lends itself less favourably than
any other of Browne's books to the process of quota-
tion. It is a pity that he did not allow himself to
expatiate on his experiments and describe more freely
some of his personal adventures in the world of nature.
We find, however, in the course of the chapter about
the whale of Hunstanton, a passage which is more
characteristic than usual, and we may give part of it
as a favourable example of the manner of the book: —

"Had the abominable scent permitted, inquiry had been
made into that strange composure of the head, and hillock of
flesh about it. Since the workmen affirmed, they met with
spermaceti before they came to the bone, and the head yet
preserved seems to confirm the same. . . . What figure the
stomach maintained in this animal of one jaw of teeth [might

have been examined], since in porpoises, which abound in both, the ventricle is trebly divided, and since in that formerly taken nothing was found but weeds and a loligo [a small cuttlefish]. . . . In vain was it to rake for ambergreece in the paunch of this Leviathan, as Greenland discoverers and attests of experience declare that they sometimes swallow great lumps thereof in the sea, insufferable fœtor denying that inquiry. And yet if, as Paracelsus encourageth, ordure makes the best musk, and from the most fetid substances may be drawn the most odoriferous essences, all that had not Vespasian's nose might boldly swear, here was a subject fit for such extractions." [1]

The way in which the mind of Browne worked in presence of a popular opinion may be followed, too, in his treatment of various quadrupeds which came under his notice in the Eastern Counties. It was generally believed, and stated in books of natural history which carried considerable authority, that the legs of the badger are longer on the right side than on the left, and that therefore he cannot run with ease until he gets on the side of a hill or the slope of a rut. No one has suggested a more reasonable source for this delusion than that, as the legs of the badger are very short and his harsh coat of fur very long, he seems, as he shambles along on his plantigrade feet, to repeat the unevenness of the ground he covers. The absurdity

---

[1] By the side of these remarks may be placed Browne's correspondence with Dr. Arthur Bacon of Yarmouth, and a passage in his posthumous writings, describing the stranding and cutting up of a whale in 1652. He held correspondence on a similar subject with Sir Hamon L'Estrange in 1653 and with Dr. Merrett in 1669. In *Religio Medici*, Browne had spoken scornfully of whales, as "prodigious pieces of nature" at pictures of which ruder heads than his might stand amazed; but we see that he became deeply excited when they actually rolled before him in their blubber on the strands of Norfolk.

of giving him legs longer on the right side than the
left, in order that he might be level as he hurries along
a slope, would be obvious, one would think, to any one
who realises that if the badger had to run over the
same ground in the opposite direction, nothing could
save him from turning heels over head.   It is characteristic of Browne that he takes no such rude short-cut
to knowledge as this.   He has to deprecate Albertus
Magnus and to shield himself behind Aldrovandi,
before he can make up his mind that the theory is
repugnant "to the three determinators of truth,
authority, sense, and reason."   He argues with great
prolixity that, although frogs and spiders have legs of
unequal length, the inequality is between pairs and
" opposite joints of neighbour-legs "; that Aristotle
has held an odd leg to be repugnant to the course of
nature; and that the argument from the lobster, whose
" chely or great claw " is larger on one side than on
the other, cannot be applied to the badger, because
the purpose of the members of the latter is progres-
sion and of the former apprehension.

Meanwhile, we cannot help asking ourselves why
the learned sceptic did not immediately get hold of a
real badger, and measure his legs.   He says that " upon
indifferent inquiry, I cannot discover this difference "
in the length of them; but why did he not make sure
for himself?   It is true that badgers are extremely
shy and mysterious in their movements, and that, no
doubt, it was not every sportsman in the neighbour-
hood of Norwich who could boast of having dug one
out of its earth.   It is perhaps to ask too much for us
to wish that, in the zeal of his zoology, Thomas Browne
himself, with a sack and a pair of badger-tongs, and

accompanied by some trusty yokels and a cross-bred bull-terrier used to the business, should have worried the bowels of earth in some copse on a starlight night, and have procured a badger for himself. But, surely, an observer so curious might have bargained with some farmer who lived out Catton way, or close to a snug rabbit-warren under Earlham, for a specimen of so common an animal. He comes to the correct conclusion, that the monstrosity is ill-contrived, "the shortness being affixed unto the legs of one side, which might have been more tolerably placed upon the thwart or diagonial movers." Quite so; but how briefly the question might have been settled once for all with a tape measure on the dead body of a badger.[1]

Browne is more experimental when he comes to the discussion of whether moles, or "molls," have eyes. Here he had himself examined specimens, and had anatomised them too, finding their eyes to be fully developed. He had kept a mole in a glass case with a toad and a viper, and had seen that it killed both these reptiles and devoured a good part of each of them. He had personally observed how hard it is to keep moles alive out of the earth; and he had noticed the extraordinary frenzy of ferocity or greed with which these little velvety beings fling themselves on their prey. He understood the character of their food, and had followed their movements and habits. It is

---

[1] This was actually done by his son, Dr. Edward Browne, who notes in his diary that, on the 10th of February 1664, he dissected a badger. As he was then living in his father's house in Norwich, we may suppose that the author of the *Vulgar Errors* assisted at this demonstration.

interesting to notice how clearly he speaks when, as
in this chapter about moles, or "molls," he is talking of
what he knows from personal observation. There is
no reference to ancient writers here; but, the moment
he gets away from his own experience, a sort of intellectual timidity seizes him. If Sammonicus has said
something absurd about the water-rat, and if Nicander
has libelled the shrew-mouse, Browne offers no resistance, because he has no personal knowledge of shrews
or water-rats; but about the mole he defies every one,
even Nonnus himself. Why, in a land of roads and
rivers, he was content to know nothing of water-rats
and shrews, it is beyond our powers to conjecture.
But it was part of Browne's character; he was less a
man of science, an all-round naturalist, than a dreamer
of philosophic dreams, satisfied with brief and partial
experiences.

We have an amusing instance of this, when Browne
comes to discourse on vulgar errors concerning the
swan. In the preceding generation a tremendous
controversy had been carried on by those two pontiffs
of the higher scholarship, Scaliger and Cardan, on the
great question whether swans do, or do not, sing as
their death is approaching. Cardan affirmed that they
invariably do; Scaliger threw contempt on such
Grecian mendacities. Both of them applied to Ælian,
whose oracle seems to have given forth an uncertain
sound. But Cardan produced the support of Pliny,
which Scaliger immediately upset by reference to
" Myndius in Athenæus." In the midst of this rever-
beration, Aldrovandi reported that dying swans had
been heard to sing, quite recently, "on the river of
Thames, near London." One would imagine that the

poems of Spenser must have reached Bologna, and have been misquoted : —

> " Two swans of goodly hue,
> Come softly swimming down along the lee, . . .
> Sweet Thames, run softly, till they end their song."

But the question of the swan-song, seriously involved by discussions as to "the serpentine and trumpet recurvation" of the bird's windpipe, and how it descendeth first into "a capsulary reception of the breast-bone," excited Browne to an unusual degree. It is amusing to note that, instead of referring at once to the everyday experiences of sailors and fishermen, or of those whose business it was to herd swans on the winding expanses of the Bure, he approaches the matter in the following transcendental manner. Nothing can be more characteristic of the temper of the man than this romantic exercise on the flutes and soft recorders of style : —

" And first from great antiquity, and before the melody of sirens, the musical note of swans hath been commended, and that they sing most sweetly before their death. For thus we read in Plato, that from the opinion of *metempsychosis*, or transmigration of the soul of men into the bodies of beasts most suitable unto their human condition, after his death, Orpheus the musician became a swan. Thus was it the bird of Apollo, the god of music, by the Greeks ; and an hieroglyphic of music among the Egyptians, from whom the Greek derived the conception ; hath been the affirmation of many Latins ; and hath not wanted assertors almost from every nation."

But he comes back to his experience at last. He seems to have dissected swans, with whose anatomy he displays considerable familiarity, and he has made wide

inquiry from prosaic persons of credit. The song of
the dying swan, he decides, is a vulgar error, and we
must abandon it; but in the very act of doing so, he
gathers his purple robes about him again, and this is
how he dismisses it : —

"When, therefore, we consider the dissention of the authors,
the falsity of relations, the indisposition of the organs, and the
immusical note of all we ever beheld or heard of; if generally
taken and comprehending all swans, we cannot assent thereto.
Surely he that is bit with a tarantula shall never be cured by
this music; and with the same hopes we expect to hear the
harmony of the spheres."

This must be held to be an instance, however, of
Browne's tendency, in his wish to multiply instances,
to slay errors that were slain before. Philemon
Holland (1601), in his version of Pliny, had plainly
laid it down that those speak "untruly" that " say
that swans sing lamentably a little before their death,
for experience in many hath shown the contrary."
Browne had the excuse of being able to give an anatomical exposition of the absurdity, but long before
his time the coronach of the wild swan had become
the exclusive property of the poets.

He had told us in *Religio Medici* how fond he was
of investigating the smaller parts of nature, and we
find him curious far beyond his age about insects
and molluscs and animalcules. The glow-worm, as
may well be supposed, had greatly excited the fancy
of the superstitious. There must always be, to rustics
and to children, something mysterious, if not miraculous, about those waxing and waning lamps of soft
green radiance, alive in the dark grasses of a summer
night. Browne's contemporaries believed that the

light of the glow-worm was perpetual, and that
luminous waters could be distilled from it. Browne
caught glow-worms and kept them alive on fresh turf
for eighteen days, closely examining through that time
the character of their light. He observed that it was
not suffused all over the body of the insect, but proceeded from "a small white part near the tail," from
whence "there ariseth a flame of a circular figure and
emerald-green colour." Of those which he kept in
captivity, he notes that, "as they declined and the
luminous humour dried, their light grew languid and
at last went out with their lives." He kept spiders in
a glass with a toad, in order to test the legend that
these creatures mutually poison each other. But there
was no poisoning. What happened was that the spiders
ran about over the body of the toad and sat upon its
head. At last, "upon advantage," he swallowed seven
of them, and afterwards dined heartily on bees, in
neither case suffering from any inconvenience. In the
course of an examination of vulgar errors about grasshoppers, Browne examined those curious masses of
foam and froth which country people call "cuckoo-
spit," and made a close investigation of the little
bright-green, cicada-like insects which inhabit them
in a larval state. The fact is, that Brown conducted
minute investigations of this humble kind far more
vigorously than he did examinations of the huge and
pompous parts of the animal creation.

For the naturalist of the early seventeenth century,
the series of recognised heraldic monsters possessed a
dangerous fascination. To deny their existence was
almost impossible, in the face of the fact that Holy
Scripture seemed to give a direct confirmation of it. It

required a very bold spirit to question the validity of
the cockatrice, when the prophet Isaiah had spoken of
hatching its eggs; and to have doubts about dragons,
when they are described so freely in the Psalms of
David.   A name was a name; the suggestion of a mis-
translation was not very kindly accepted in circles
which were accustomed to believe in the plenary
inspiration of an English Bible.   The griffin was a
beast which gave Browne a great deal of trouble.
The fore part of him was that of an eagle, with wings
and a hooked beak, but the flanks, hind-legs, and tail
were those of a lion.   Browne decides, on the whole,
that the idea of this creature is symbolical, and that
it does not exist in nature.   Aldrovandi "hath in a
large discourse rejected" the griffin, and this is a help
to our philosophic doubter.   But "many affirm, and
most (I perceive) deny not," and the griffin presents a
great deal of difficulty.   We are grieved to find a too-
constant harking back to "the testimonies of ancient
writers," to sculpture, where the monster has held a
splendid sway, and to poetry, where he still outspeeds
the Arimaspian.

On the whole, however, and in face of all these
respectable witnesses, Browne is inclined firmly to
repudiate the griffin.   He finds the raw conjunction
of bird and beast shocking to his biological instincts,
and though for a moment he is shaken by the analogy
of the bat (which he evidently supposed to be half-
beast, half-bird), he decides that in that case there is
a commixture of both kinds running through the
species, " so confirmed and set together that he cannot
define the beginning or end of either."   It is the
crudity of the griffin, as of two fragments abruptly

cemented together, that shocks him. So the wyvern, the front of which is a winged dragon and the back a serpent, affronts nature by its violence. Browne saw that these direct anomalies disturbed the laws of nature, but his arguments were singularly primitive and timid. How could he, who had prosecuted so much anatomy, and who was so familiar with the interior economy of beasts and birds, not ask himself whether, in the frame of the griffin, the viscera of an eagle could suddenly join those of a lion without absolute discord and disparity of instinct? He finally decides that such creatures as the wyvern and the griffin are symbolical and enigmatical, but he does not grip the fable and fling it, as we expect him to do.

The phœnix he treats more bravely, and dismisses it on the score of the absence of all ocular testimony. We learn, accidentally, that he had never seen other than feathers of the famous Eastern bird of paradise, of which he tells us that the janizaries of Constantinople made, in his day, "their ordinary plume," just as vain and selfish ladies in ours permit the egret to be destroyed that a tremulous spray of feathers may quiver above their bonnets. Curious legends about the salamander are still familiar to modern readers, although few people now believe that if thrown upon the hearth it extinguishes the fire like ice, or that it can continue to live in flames. More extraordinary to us sounds the notion that out of the wool of salamanders can be woven a kind of cloth which resists the action of fire. To shave a salamander strikes one as the most hopeless industry to which a man could possibly addict himself, and even Browne, who never smiles, contends that it must be "a fallacious enlarge-

ment" which speaks of napkins woven from the wool
of "a kind of lizard, a quadruped corticated and
depilous." To the indestructible character of the skin
of the salamander, he objects that Brassavolus got hold
of one dead, and did successfully burn it. Browne
hints, but hesitates to say in so many words, that what
the ancients called a salamander was really a newt or
water-lizard. There is always the curious little lurk-
ing trepidation that, in denying these old stories of
monsters, the scientific reformer may be committing
an act of impiety.

Browne suffered from the circumstance that most of
those who had preceded him in description of the
animal world had written, as he says, poetically or
mystically or enigmatically or hermetically or rhetorically, but not, as we should put it to-day, biologically.
They made no attempt to interpret structure in relation
to the life-history of an animal or a class of animals ;
but if something ridiculously inept was reported of it,
they gave the report, which might be a mere piece
of heraldic symbolism, the benefit of the doubt.
A very curious instance was the persistent belief in
the basilisk or cockatrice, a creature which combined
the peculiarities of a mammal, a bird, and a reptile.
It was imagined with a beast's legs, dragon's wings,
serpentine and winding tail, and the comb of a cock.
It was supposed to be the offspring of a cock's egg
hatched under a toad. Browne did not feel that he
"could safely deny" that some animal of this kind
might exist, and he would doubtless have been exceedingly nonplussed if a specimen of that lively little
reptile, the mitred iguana of Mexico, had been presented to his notice. But he is bold to deny the story

of the eggs hatched under a toad, which he styles
"a conceit as monstrous as the brood itself," and he
very properly suggests that many of the fantastic
stories about basilisks are purely symbolic, or, as he
puts it, hieroglyphical.

What was the most preposterous legend about this
monster, however, is dealt with by Browne very
timidly. The ancients believed that the basilisk could
kill an enemy from a distance by the mere flash of
light from its eye-ball; "this venenation shooteth
from the eye." Does not the Lady Anne say to
Gloster, when he praises her eyes, "Would they were
basilisks to strike thee dead"? Browne found no
difficulty in believing that the visible ray might carry
forth the subtlest part of a poison, and that this could
not act unless it were seen by the victim. You might
walk through a forest, with basilisks fulminating from
every bough, but you suffered no harm at all from
these venomous ejections, unless you were imprudent
enough to meet a basilisk eye to eye, in which case
you departed this life in great agony. It is evident
that Browne's conception of optics was still in its
infancy. It appears that sailors and travellers were in
the habit of bringing the skins of basilisks home with
them from the tropics; Browne speaks of these as "artificial impostures," but we may question whether they
were not in some instances the skins of such iguanoid
saurians as we have mentioned above. Very effective
basilisks, however, could be constructed out of the
dried bodies of thornback-rays, with their immense
breadth of fin and winding snaky tail. Browne
seems to indicate that he has exercised his own ingenuity in counterfeiting such basilisks.

In the fourth book of the *Vulgar Errors,* Browne
deals with many popular and received tenets respecting
the human body, which he examines or proves either
false or dubious. Here his long practical experience
as a surgeon helps him. It seems very curious that
the position of the heart should be generally unknown
in the seventeenth century, but we gather from Browne
that the "careless and inconsiderate aspection" of
anatomists had betrayed popular judgment into believing it to lie much more to the left side than it
really does. Many of the errors which he exposes are
of a superstitious kind, as that drowned men's bodies
rise on the ninth day, and that sneezing has a ritual
significance. These ideas have long ceased to be held
by such readers as Browne addressed, although some
of them still find currency with the unthinking. What
Browne says about Jews is extraordinarily rude, and
his Hebrew readers, if he had any, must have com-
plained that it was more painful to be defended by
such an advocate than to be left to the casual obloquy
of the vulgar. He does not absolutely deny that there
may be a race of pigmies somewhere, but he cannot
believe that when they gallop to battle against cranes
they ride upon the backs of partridges.

The fifth book deals with the injury which has been
done to the judgment of credulous persons by the preposterous fancy of people who have drawn pictures out
of their own heads. Here, no doubt, the symbolical
and the heraldic elements came in and disturbed the
simple-minded. There were the monsters of Gothic
imagination, the goblins and supporters of cathedrals
and coats of arms ; it was easy for an irresponsible illus-
trator to copy a gargoyle and say that he had drawn

it from the life in some sequestered valley of Arabia.
There were certain zoological types of fallacy, of which
the pelican in her piety, opening her breast that she
might feed her young ones with her blood, was a prominent example.   Browne, who was familiar with real
pelicans, was able to correct the picture-makers.   He
gives a full and accurate description of this remarkable
bird, which the illustrators painted green or yellow
instead of white, and with a short bill, instead of with
the long mandible, carrying a capacious bag attached,
which is so familiar in our aviaries.   Browne was no
less indignant at the conventional pictures of the
dolphin, which in his day represented that cetacean
"convexedly crooked" or else "concavously inverted,"
clasped around an anchor or writhing to dislocation in
the ecstasy of carrying Arion.

It does not seem, however, from the observations
which he makes in the course of the *Vulgar Errors* that
Browne had formed any true conceptions of a zoological
character.   In this he was not before his time.   The
anatomical and physiological character of the medical
studies he had pursued at Padua had quickened his
curiosity in natural objects, and had encouraged in him
the temper of inquiry.   But at the moment in which
Browne lived, the phenomena of animal life, whether
of form or function, were still unexplained by the laws
of physics and of chemistry, and it is this absence of
explanation which makes itself felt in all the vague
opinions of the *Vulgar Errors*.   It is particularly to
be remembered that the microscope had not yet been
brought to the aid of anatomical research; when
Browne's book saw the light, Anton van Leeuwenhoek
was but a boy of seventeen.   The physician of Norwich

lived, as I have said, on the very frontier of the
promised land, but he never crossed it. We may take
as an example the chapter "Of Lampries." The error
which he contends against here is that the lamprey
has seven (Browne, like the German language, says
nine) eyes on each side behind its head. Browne
saw that "it were a superfluous inartificial act to
place and settle so many in one place." In point
of fact he came very near to the truth, which is
that these cavities form a row of bronchiai openings,
through which water is permitted to permeate the
gills. He had seen the lamprey spurt water through
"a fistula or pipe at the back part of the head"; he
observed, but it was with an uncertain and unaided
vision. In the same way, he discourses of the eyes of
snails, and here he speaks of information said to have
been gained by others with the "help of exquisite
glasses," which he has, it is evident, not obtained.
Inability to take advantage of the microscope is
plainly responsible for the main part of Browne's
imperfections.

It is proper, therefore, that we should not be led
away by our affection for Browne, and by his charming
way of saying things, to exaggerate the scientific value
of the *Vulgar Errors*. That value seems to be small.
There is something very entertaining in the repetition
of monstrous tales about animals, and plants, and
minerals ; but it would be a mistake to think that
these tales, or even their refutation, influenced the
course of knowledge. Professor Ray Lankester says —
and his words may be directly applied to such writers
as Browne — "whilst the theories and fables which
were current in earlier times in regard to animal life

and the various kinds of animals form an important subject of study from the point of view of the development of the human mind, they really have no bearing upon the history of scientific zoology." Browne, for whom the very conception of what we call zoology had not separated itself from a general "physiology," or vague, unrelated curiosity concerning the phenomena of nature, is interesting as a writer, even as a moralist, but not as a pioneer in science. He is not one of those who, from Edward Wotton to Ray, down a century of ardent endeavour, drew the veil more and more completely away from the mysteries of animal life. With all his pleasant energy, with all his zeal against " false representations," Browne was contented to preserve a condition of mental life into which the spirit of severe inquiry had not yet intruded. It was to set in, a very few years later, with the advent of the Royal Society.

The *Vulgar Errors* is a work so discursive that criticism will doubtless do best to treat it in a wholly desultory way. We may find it most instructive to begin by amusing ourselves with all its odd digressions, speculation of what maggots naturally signify, of the causes of the long life of crows, of whether the gall of the deer is seated in its liver or its guts. We may like to turn the cheerful pages vaguely, and learn why dogs can search out a Jew in the dark, and what " fuliginous efflorescences and complexional tinctures " cause the negro to be black. But when we are satiated with all such questions as these, and tired of the ineffectual dogmatism of the whole book, — so vain nowadays, when our hand-books and our encyclopædias are ready to tell us the precise facts about such matters, — then

we shall do well to return to the opening chapters of
the *Vulgar Errors*, and see what was Browne's philosophical aim in composing it. In the first place, then,
by the light of those chapters we see that the *Pseudodoxia Epidemica*, to give it its pompous title, is designed, in Pater's admirable definition, to be "a criticism, a cathartic, an instrument for the clarifying of
the intellect." To attain that end the author begins
by defining and accounting for man's liability to gross
error, his strange "deceivability in his perfection."

Browne finds that all created beings, yes, even
"the angels of light in all their clarity," are naturally
subject to error. The source of all the mistakes of
reported observation with which he proposes to deal
is this fallible nature of man, for which he accounts by
supposing that there exists in us all an inborn tendency to see things and to remember things as they
are not, an erroneous inclination of the mind. He has
been very much impressed, in the course of his medical
experience, by the fact that most persons, when brought
face to face with the truth, are unable to appreciate it.
They look at a badger, and simply because they have
formed a preconceived impression that its legs are
shorter on one side than on the other, they think that
what they see before them confirms them in their
belief. They are "bad discoverers of verity," because
they do not allow their senses to have full sway, but
are drawn aside, as by a set of malignant magnets, by
the "perverted apprehensions and conceptions of the
world." We may allow Browne to dilate at some
length on this view of the causes of error, since it
contains the central idea round which the loose texture
of the *Vulgar Errors* is woven. He has been speaking

of those who cannot see a natural truth when it lies
patent before their vision : —

"Moreover, their understanding, thus weak in itself, and
perverted by sensible delusions, is yet further impaired by the
dominion of their appetite ; that is, the irrational and brutal
part of the soul, which, lording it over the sovereign faculty,
interrupts the actions of that noble part, and chokes those
tender sparks which Adam hath left them of reason. And
therefore they do not only swarm with errors, but vices de-
pending thereon. Thus they commonly affect no man any
further than he deserts his reason, or complies with their
aberrancies. Hence they embrace not virtue for itself, but
its reward ; and the argument from pleasure or utility is far
more powerful than that from virtuous honesty, which Ma-
homet and his contrivers well understood, when he set out
the felicity of his heaven, by the contentments of flesh, and the
delights of sense, slightly passing over the accomplishment
of the soul, and the beatitude of that part which earth and visi-
bilities too weakly affect. But the wisdom of our Saviour and
the simplicity of his truth proceeded another way, defying the
popular provisions of happiness from sensible expectations,
placing his felicity in things removed from sense, and the
intellectual enjoyment of God. And therefore the doctrine
of the one was never afraid of universities, or endeavoured the
banishment of learning, like the other. And though Galen
doth sometimes nibble at Moses . . . yet is there surely no
reasonable Pagan that will not admire the rational and well-
grounded precepts of Christ."

The subjugation of the writer's will to the precepts
of revealed religion is hardly less manifest here than
it was in each alternate page of *Religio Medici*. In
later chapters, Browne expands his view in the winding
way that he always prefers to adopt, but he goes no
further in scepticism than to suggest that holy writers
have used expressions which were fitted rather to the
apprehension of their readers than to positive veracity

or the exact nature of things. Some of the examples
he quotes are of a trivial nature, as when he reminds
us that Solomon's molten sea was said to be three
times its diameter in circumference, whereas it ought
to have been a fraction more. But he finds a better
instance when he points out that the sun and the
moon are termed the two great lights of heaven,
although the moon is now known to be an almost
insignificant satellite. Here Scripture " omitteth the
exact account " of the phenomena, " describing them
rather to our apprehensions." But, of course, there is
no such thing as an absolute conception of truth, and
Browne is illogical, or not quite sincere, when he puts
the describing of the moon as a great light — which in
our hemisphere it unquestionably is — on a level with
the statement that the wearing of an amethyst will
prevent a man from getting drunk, which is true in
no age or climate.

If, however, Browne did not quite perceive that
truth is an ideal which cannot be realised, and obscured his own sense of symbolical or relative truth
by seeking after positive formulas, at least he saw
the value of negation. It is a very great matter, in
dealing with a mass of spurious statement, to be able
boldly to deny the fact. This Browne did, often with
a great deal of courage, and he ought to have this
credit. This is, indeed, the answer to those who
say that he himself made as many mistakes as his
forerunners. He did not make so many; and those
he did make were new, and therefore transient, with
no dangerous tradition behind them. The great merit
of the *Vulgar Errors*, as a contribution to contemporary thought, was that it took a long series of

pragmatical assertions about phenomena, and showed
that they broke down in face of experience. Like
Cardan, learned men had "taken some things upon
trust, and although they examined some, they had
let slip many others." The ancient writers, Browne
still thought, were "of singular use unto a prudent
reader," but he faced the necessity of asserting, with
more or less firmness as his courage rose or fell, that
in a great many specific instances, these ancients, with
all their parade of depth and latitude of learning, were,
on demonstration, wrong.

In his famous *History of Civilisation* (1857), Buckle
started a theory regarding the development of scepticism in the seventeenth century, which he illustrated
mainly by the example of Browne. Buckle's idea was
that we may trace an extraordinary step forward in
the emancipation of the human mind by comparing
the *Vulgar Errors* with *Religio Medici*. In the latter, Buckle thought that he found evidence of an
almost mediæval credulity; the author of it was still
bound hand and foot to tradition, and gloried in
asserting the perfect humility of his faith. He was a
complete instance of that "superiority over, or neglect
of inquiry," which the new science was to reprove and
awaken. In the *Vulgar Errors*, although published but
six years later, Buckle finds an entirely different
temper of intellect. " But for the most decisive evidence," he says, "we could hardly believe it to be
written by the same man" who wrote *Religio Medici*.
On this theme the historian of civilisation builds
quite an imposing critical structure. He believes that
in those few years Browne had changed his whole
character, and had adopted an attitude to science and

religion, the tone " of which is inconsistent with the
old theological spirit." Browne is now as eager to
expose the blunders of the Fathers as he was before
insistent in bowing down to them and accepting them.
Buckle attributes it to the effect of the Revolution
and the Civil War upon a mind of great ductility,
which had suddenly become awakened to the fact
that religion was trading upon the credulity of
man.

This plausible and interesting theory, however, is
one which breaks down, like some fable of Oppian or
Albertus Magnus, before a close examination of the
books themselves. It is, perhaps, not unkind to surmise that Buckle read his *Vulgar Errors* rather
eclectically than exhaustively. He read, seeking for
confirmation of a theory he had already formed. The
sinuous methods of Browne are particularly capable
of betraying such a student; for, indeed, by quoting a
passage from any one of his books without reference
to the context, it would be easy to surmise that he
must have been an atheist and a fanatic, an eager
seeker into truth, and a superstitious ignoramus. He
pursues his leisurely and winding way, and we must
always read enough of him to ensure perception of
the long trend of his argument. If we do this, I do
not think we shall arrive at the conclusion that the
author of *Religio Medici* differed in anything essential
from the author of the *Vulgar Errors*. In each book
Browne shows himself the same, a man of piety who
did not wish his faith to be obscured by unnecessary
and slavish excesses of credulity; who felt to the
inmost fibre of his being the mystery and the
solemnity of life, but did not choose in its contempla-

tion to lose his self-control; a man who dreaded exaggeration and emphasis, who loved a moderate liberty of mental action, and who wished to be master of his own soul without oppressing or offending his neighbour.

The *Pseudodoxia Epidemica* was well received, although with little of the cosmopolitan enthusiasm which had greeted *Religio Medici*. Alexander Ross came forward again to the attack, with an *Arcana Microcosmi* (1652), in which he tried to put some of the old monsters, which Browne had turned out, back into their places; but Ross was growing elderly and stupid, and his old-fashioned pamphlet passed almost unobserved. A like fate befell the animadversions contained in the *Eudoxa* (1656) of John Robinson, another bolt shot out of the old camp, which was little noticed in its original Latin form, and still less in its English version of 1658. Those who are inclined to smile at Browne's occasional and partial credulity should glance at the gross pages of Ross and Robinson; Browne will appear to them, by contrast, to have been an angel of scientific light. James Windet, a young physician settled in Yarmouth, seems to have been a disciple of Browne's and to have formed the design of producing a panegyric on the *Vulgar Errors*. Windet's letters to Browne have never been published, but they passed through the hands of Simon Wilkin, who has described them as "most tedious and pedantick, — written in Latin, profusely ornamented with Greek and even Arabick, but utterly destitute of interest." No gold dust there, it is evident, for the impoverished biographer of Browne, nor any sparkle of it in the five letters preserved among the Robinson Manuscripts from one Isaac Gruter,[1] dated between 1650 and 1675, and dealing languidly with a proposal that the writer should translate the *Vulgar Errors* into Latin; this project it does not appear that he ever carried out. All that these desultory facts give us is evidence of the position of Browne in the literary world, and the respect which his accomplishments awakened.

The popular success of the *Vulgar Errors* exposed its author to a curious annoyance. In 1657 a London publisher, Edward Farnham, was impertinent enough to issue a book called *Nature's Cabinet Unlock'd*, which he attributed on the title-page to "Tho. Brown D. of Physick." That this was a deliberate fraud, and not an accident or a similarity of name, is proved by the preface, in the course of which certain published phrases of our author are woven into the text, while at the foot are printed, in large letters like a signature, the words "Religio Medici." Browne was so much annoyed that, in issuing a protest in 1658, he said that since "either he must write himself, or others will write for him," he "knew no better prevention than to act his own part with less intermission of his pen," and it seems therefore that we owe to the forgery of *Nature's Cabinet Unlock'd* the publication of those precious works which will occupy us in the following chapter. The scandalous little production itself is an elementary treatise of "physiology," in the seventeenth century sense, a handbook to miscellaneous knowledge about gems and plants, spirits and metals, and all kinds of animate and inanimate bodies.

[1] Isaac Gruter was probably one of the "three or four sons, who were all scholars," of the eccentric and perambulatory Dutch physician, Pieter Gruter of Dixmuid, who died in 1634.

CHAPTER IV

URN-BURIAL AND *THE GARDEN OF CYRUS*

(1658)

THE absence of almost all allusion to the Civil War in the writings and correspondence of Thomas Browne is an instance of what has often been commented upon, the narrowly localised effect of great political struggles in the seventeenth century.   Browne lived in the city of Norwich from a time long before the breaking out of the war until a time when the war had become almost forgotten, and nothing in his works would lead us to suppose that he ever had any personal cognisance of it.   Norfolk was an eminently Puritan county, and tainted both with indifferentism and with hostility to the Establishment.   In the year when Browne took up his abode in Norwich, it was reported to Laud that " the cathedral church is much out of order ; the hangings of the choir are naught, the pavement not good, the spire of the steeple is quite down, the churchyard is very ill kept."   There was a general coolness about conformity, and when the outbreak came, Norfolk accepted the change of government very complacently. Norwich was fortified in the Cromwellian interest, and presently settled down to its affairs with an easy negligence of national ambitions.

Browne was a staunch royalist by conviction all his life, but curiously enough the only act by which we know that he displayed his opinions was a passive one, which exposed him to no inconvenience. When the king's army took Newcastle in the summer of 1642, the blow seemed serious to the Parliament, and after a while a fund was raised to try to regain this fortress. Browne was one of some four hundred citizens of Norwich who, on being invited to contribute for this purpose, begged to decline their mite. As a royalist, he could really do no less, but this is the boldest stroke for his king that our ardent royalist is known to have made. It is highly probable, however, that his private action, if not heroic, was extremely useful to the cause. The royalists of Norfolk, at first in a hopeless minority, strengthened one another by private advices, and confidentially added so many adherents to their number, that at the Restoration no county in England welcomed the king with greater ardour. Browne's practice lay among the best county families, the Bacons, the L'Estranges, the Pastons, and their fellows; and he would have many opportunities of fortifying his patients in their faith and encouraging them, with his unfailing optimism, to look forward to a good time coming.

Optimism was sometimes needful, especially in 1648, when a wild blast of political hysteria blew through Norwich, culminating in what always remained an incident as mysterious as dreadful, when in the midst of a riot the Committee House was blown up and more than one hundred persons killed, accidentally, as was alleged. In this same year two women were put to death for witchcraft in Norwich:

one hopes our *medicus* was not responsible for that.
This was the darkest time of the unfortunate city,
which fell into great destitution, and in 1649, on the
plea of great loss and decay of trade, and general
poverty of all classes, made a pitiful appeal to Parliament to abate the taxes.

As the years rolled on, almost noiselessly, we fancy,
over the heads of the serene and affectionate family in
Norwich, the doctor himself insensibly grew to be a
great figure in the town.   At all events, he became a
figure which persons with scientific and literary tastes,
gazing at Norwich from a distance, saw rising higher
and higher above those of the other citizens.   He
became an object of worship to young disciples and
remote admirers.   We know that he was not facetious
nor a merry companion; his talk was grave, perhaps
continuous; we form an image of him as peripatetic
in the cathedral close, with one, or at most two, serious
young men, walking at his side and listening to his
flow of conversation.   We know, too, that he had a
rare genius for friendship, and it displayed itself in a
warm and tender sympathy for those younger than
himself.   "I love my friend," he wrote, "before
myself, and yet methinks I do not love him enough.
Some few months hence my multiplied affection will
make me believe I have not loved him at all."   This
comes out in the fragments of his correspondence.
A young disciple comes to stay with him in Norwich,
and departs laden with good things of the spirit,
stimulated, strengthened, uplifted.   But Browne broods
over the memory of his visit, and thinks he has not
done enough for his friend, and writes a solemn
buckram letter of still further advice and help, in

which we daily see the yearning affection, the belief that "I have not loved him at all," under the sententious language.

They rewarded him with adoration, these children of his spirit. They sunned themselves in the warmth of his "sublime solid fancy." His books were carried about under their cloaks, with a little confidential pressure of the arm against the body, as though to say "there he is." One of the disciples, writing from a distance, tells Browne that he "hugs your Minerva to his bosom, and votes it his *vade mecum*." The young men found in his talk "more varieties and delights than all the folios and book-follies of the time could afford" them. His advice was grave and magisterial. He told them, as he told Henry Power, to lay their foundation in anatomy, "wherein *autopsia* must be your *fidus Achates*." He told them, since almost all of them were physicists, to attend operations whenever they could, to see what chemists do in their *officines*, and to seek with all their might to peer further and further into the mysteries of nature. He extolled upon every occasion the great use of Greek in all branches of physic, and he did not weary of asserting that "without Greek nothing can be done to perfection." He preferred Harvey's discovery of the circulation of the blood far beyond that of Columbus; and saw no great reason for exploring new worlds while we were still so ignorant of the old world which lies about us.

Total strangers would write from distant places to say that they should hold themselves eternally obliged if the worthy and right worshipful doctor would "condescend so low" as to advise them about their

course of reading. These letters would sometimes lead
to friendships, for Browne would be struck by some
ardour of intelligence, and would invite the writer to
visit him at Norwich. So, in the winter of 1648,
Henry Power — a graduate of Christ's College, who
had been at Cambridge, working at science, since
1641, but who deplored "such few helps" to it there
— came over and lived a month or two in Norwich
to be close to Browne. Power became, perhaps, the
most beloved of all the disciples; the doctor gave
him a great deal of his attention, showed him, as
Hood's schoolboy might have said, a viper's fangs and
everything that could make him comfortable. He
taught him " to simple," that is to say, to botanise in
the woods, meadows, and fields, and to such good
purpose that when Power went back to college, he
simpled at Cambridge, and going out three or four
miles once a week soon collected between two and
three hundred species of plants. Nothing seems to
have pleased Browne more than that his young men
should devote themselves to botany; he himself was
always haunted by memories of the plant-garden of
Monsieur Chicaneau in Montpellier, when the Judas-
tree used to be crimson with blossom in May.

Power introduced to Browne another scientist of
Christ's, Thomas Smith, and the men conceived the
daring plan of inviting the celebrated naturalist to Cambridge, and putting him up in College. If he accepted
their offer, it must have been in the winter of 1648–9,
but unhappily no record of such an interesting visit
exists. In 1649 Power took a practice at Halifax, where
his family seem to have known Browne in earlier years.
The friendship continued till Power's death in 1668;

he did not leave much behind him, but he was a careful "experimental philosopher," and is remembered as one of the two earliest elected fellows of the Royal Society, an honour never bestowed upon his master. Thomas Smith became University Librarian in 1659, and died in 1661. He was a learned and pugnacious theologian, who disputed publicly in Cambridge against George Fox and the Quakers, and who attacked Bunyan.[1]

All the best people of the old society seem to have been Browne's patients at Norwich. He used to go out to Heigham, to the little house where the deposed bishop, that noble relic of the Elizabethan age, Joseph Hall — his cathedral desecrated and his revenues sequestrated — spent in painful obscurity the last nine years of his life. To soothe and attend the failing age of this "notorious delinquent" exhibited very plainly the sentiments of the physician, and Browne showed courage in his charge of Bishop Hall, who survived under his care until the 29th of May 1656. In 1650 another very staunch royalist, Sir Hamon L'Estrange of Hunstanton, met with the *Vulgar Errors*, delighted in it, and became a patient and friend of Browne's till his death in 1660. L'Estrange was an ardent old man after Browne's own heart; he had been a great traveller, an adventurer for the North-West Passage and an explorer in Ceylon. In the very last year of his long life he drew up notes, in expansion of and commentary upon the *Vulgar Errors*, enough to form a pamphlet and almost a volume. Browne attended

---

[1] For particulars regarding Power and Smith, I have to thank the kindness of my friend Dr. John Peile, the present Master of Christ's College.

the Paston family also.   Sir William Paston, of Paston
and Castle Rising, was made high sheriff of Norfolk in
the year when the doctor arrived in Norwich; he
suffered greatly during the Commonwealth.   But it
was his son Robert, long afterwards the first Earl of
Yarmouth, who was Browne's particular friend, a
young man of parts and ambition, who, in 1655, had
just gone down from Trinity College, Cambridge.   He
had scientific tastes and was one of Browne's disciples;
it was of him that in 1657 Evelyn asked the favour of
a personal introduction to the celebrated author of
Religio Medici.

One of Browne's main interests was the collection of
antiquities, and in particular of coins found in the
course of excavations.   Such treasures turned up not
unfrequently in Norfolk, and it became the delight of
Browne's patients to gratify him by making additions
to his cabinet.   In particular Mr. Thomas Wood· of
Caistor, "a person of civility, industry, and knowledge
in this way," himself a learned antiquary, sent him a
great number of rare silver and copper coins from a
place on his estate called East Bloodyburgh Furlong,
to Browne's exceeding delight.   Various finds included,
not merely moneys, but urns, gems, and bones, and
these also, though apparently at first to a less extent,
interested Browne, who was the type of the omni-
vorous country antiquary.   At last, apparently in the
autumn of 1657, in a field at Old Walsingham, there
were turned up no fewer than between forty and fifty
urns, "deposited in a dry and sandy soil, not a yard
deep, nor far from one another."   These vessels contained human bones and ashes, as well as ornaments
of ivory and brass, and in one of them Browne

discovered a small object which he believed to be an opal.

Such finds of pottery were, as we have said, not uncommon in Norfolk in those days. Browne has recorded similar discoveries made at Brancaster, at Thorpe, at Caistor, at Burnham. The science of the day knew not how to adjust its impressions of their antiquity, nor to what period to attach them. Browne was of the confident opinion that they were all of Roman origin, and he held this to be " no obscure conjecture," but absolutely proved from various circumstances which he details. He thought these Walsingham urns in particular had formed part of the furniture of the Roman colony of Brannodunum. But in this essential and primary consideration he was in error. As Sir John Evans has pointed out, the modern antiquary has only to glance at the frontispiece to Browne's *Urn-Burial* to see that the vessels were not of Roman but of Saxon origin. We do not go to Browne to-day for correct antiquarian information — although some of his notes about coins are said to preserve their value — but as we should to the rhapsody of some great poet, to be borne along on the wind of his imaginative afflatus.

Criticism can suggest to itself few more fascinating, but few more hopeless, tasks than to determine what it was which suddenly inflamed the genius of Browne in the early months of 1658. At the age of fifty-three, a country physician, with a large practice in and around the county town, who for twelve years had abandoned the small ambition he may have once felt to shine in the profession of letters, suddenly appears to us illuminated by the sacred fire, voluble in music like Pythia

on her tripod, and pouring forth paragraph after paragraph of elaborate writing, almost any one of which
might be chosen as an example of the best English
prose writing of the seventeenth century. *Religio
Medici* had been exquisite in easy grace; the *Vulgar
Errors* had occasional passages of a picturesque kind,
buried in much that was very dull and uninspired;
the *Urn-Burial* is an imaginative exercise as audacious
as *Lycidas*, and almost as successful. That nothing
should have led up to it, that (at all events) between
1635 and 1658 there should have been no hint or
murmur of the hidden music, this is extraordinary
indeed. It is as though a brown bird should keep
silent in a cage until every one had forgotten its
existence, and then suddenly fill the darkness with
its harmony, and prove to be a nightingale.

So far as we can see, it was that supposed opal in
the urn from Walsingham which touched the spring
in Browne's brain. His fancy took hold of this little
dim jewel, if jewel indeed it was, come to light again
among the dust after so many centuries. He flew to
the conviction that it was the symbol of some far-away
romance: first he persuaded himself that it had been
burned upon the finger of the dead; next, that at the
last moment of farewell, in an agony of regret, some affectionate friend had flung it into the flames as a memorial.
It appears to me that the gorgeous texture of the *Urn-
Burial* was all woven around this opal, that the rare
dreams and singular fancies pass and return that they
may form a silken net for this questionable object,
which lies at last hidden in their golden tissue, like the
chrysalis of the silkworm in its elastic and glittering
fleece. The only way in which we can explain the

existence of *Urn-Burial,* one of the most curious and
unaccountable of books, is to suppose that this or some
similar incident inflamed the slumbering genius of its
author.   This alone accounts for the high note of
imaginative excitement, the uplifted ecstasy, which
inspires the strange treatise from the first page to
the last.

This note of sombre passion is sounded fully in the
letter which the author addressed on the 1st of May
1658 to Thomas Le Gros of Crostwick, on whose estate
important cinerary discoveries had been made.   Browne
was fascinated by the echo made in the depths of his
soul by these " sad and sepulchral pitchers, which have
no joyful voices."   Most men have at one time or
another been conscious of the sentiment which environs
prehistoric vessels drawn out of the damp earth, black
and smooth with age, dully sounding as if grown dumb
in that long sequestration.   They stand before us —
and we are now speaking, as Browne was speaking, not
of painted and sonorous urns enclosed for kings in the
vain and idle dignity of some majestic mausoleum, but
of the rustic cups and bowls of country service — these
stand before us as humble ministers of a race long
buried and forgotten.   They are messengers from the
past, but too weak and frail to transmit to us an
intelligible record.   There they are, humid with the
cold, soft earth about them, and they come direct from
the hands and lips of those who were our ancestors.
Some furtive phantom seems to escape from the pale
clay, but it is voiceless and it has vanished before we
could challenge it.   The dim life in it, so long arrested
in its subterranean prison, has given one flutter, one
pulsation, and it is dispersed for ever.

Browne's whole interest in these brown pots centred around their human associations. There was always present with him the idea that the little urns had contained, might yet contain, bones of men, the calcined remnants of those who had once walked in the Norfolk fields. These dim receptacles had served as exiguous dwelling-places for the disembodied soul, shelters against the vast continuity of nothingness. So long as they existed, something of the individual remained intact; not merely untroubled but, in some half-conscious way, satisfied and almost happy, in a dim trance of contentment. When a black urn was dug up and opened, returning, so unwillingly, to the importunate noises of the world, some pathetic essence, some sort of diluted soul, sighed itself forth upon the air, and died at last. Those who so sheltered and concealed their beloved, anticipated no such outrage upon their repose : —

" When the funeral pyre was out, and the last valediction over, men took a lasting adieu of their interred friends, little expecting the curiosity of future ages should comment upon their ashes; and, having no old experience of the duration of their relics, held no opinion of such after-considerations. But who knows the fate of his bones, or how often he is to be buried ? Who hath the oracle of his ashes, or whither they are to be scattered ? "

This is the temper in which the treatise called *Hydriotaphia: Urn-Burial* is composed. The jewelled, slow-moving sentences proceed with an impression of extraordinary gorgeousness and pomp, heavy and almost bowed down under their trappings of ornament. The problem in Browne's mind was to decide what virtue yet sleeps in those aged cinders. As this fantastic idea revolved in his mind, it took wonderful shapes of mystery and music; it branched to heaven, it pushed down into hell. The pretence of antiquarian research, of supplying definite fact regarding the particular vessels dug up at Old Walsingham, became slight indeed. One can imagine the profound dissatisfaction with which a prosaic reader, anxious to obtain information of a sociological character, and quite indifferent to the graces of Browne's style, would turn the pages of the *Urn-Burial*. Here is applicable the immortal simile of Shelley, since to go to Browne's book for plain archæological statement would indeed be like applying to a gin-shop for a shoulder of mutton. In the highly inflammable state of Browne's imagination, a phrase or epithet is sufficient to start him off, and he blazes in a spurt of odorous language, like a pine-knot touched by a lighted match. The following paragraph, as well as, but no better than, a dozen others, may serve to exemplify the quite extraordinary way in which Browne's fancy goes dreaming on, one clause taking flame from another, and the whole uplifted on the full colour and sound of the words themselves : —

" No lamps, included liquors, lachrymatories, or tear-bottles attended these rural urns, either as sacred unto the *manes*, or passionate expressions of their surviving friends. While with rich flames, and hired tears, they solemnised their obsequies, and in the most lamented monuments made one part of their inscriptions. Some find sepulchral vessels containing liquors, which time hath incrassated into jellies. For, besides these lachrymatories, notable lamps, with vessels of oils and aromatical liquors, attended noble ossuaries; and some yet retaining a vinosity and spirit in them, which, if any have tasted, they have far exceeded the palates of antiquity. Liquors not to

be computed by years of annual magistrates, but by great
conjunctions and the fatal periods of kingdoms. The draughts
of consulary date were but crude unto these, and Opimian
wine but in the must unto them."

The pursuit of the imaginative chimera could, in a
trivial way, go no further. Good wine improves by
keeping, and loses its fiery rawness in maturity.
Therefore, if it is improved by ten years' care, what
an imperial silkiness, what an indescribable gusto of
mellowness, must it not obtain after a thousand years!
It is a plain matter of the rule of three, and Browne's
imagination goes off in one flight of fancy after another
about the ecstasy which those must enjoy who are
privileged to taste a " vintage, that hath been cooled
a long age in the deep-delvèd earth." The tiresome
little fact that, after a very short time, the process is
reversed and the wine is ruined by keeping, so that
what is found in old bottles of Falernian is nothing but
a cake of acrid resin, is well within Browne's range of
observation, but he flings it indignantly away. It has
no place in the scheme of his beautiful florid vision of
a glorified vinosity.

He must not, however, be thought of as habitually
absurd. His reflections are often as sober as they are
charming. For instance, the whole of the section in
which he treats of the methods of ancient sepulture is
not merely eloquent, but moderate and reasonable.
He speaks in favour of those who are antiquaries like
himself. While others desire to pierce to the bowels
of Potosi, and rend the very structure of the earth in
their pursuit after precious metals, his friends and he,
indifferent about wealth, ask no more than to be permitted to rake an inch or two below the surface of the

soil. What they seek so eagerly, that is to say, lamps and coins and tear-bottles, lie scarce underneath the roots of plants. Indeed, as he says in one of his quick appeals to the visual sense, you may have to disengage the sides of an urn from the long roots of dog's grass, wreathed about the bones inside it. Those that are in the act to die desire that the earth should lie upon them lightly. Browne discourses very learnedly of what the practices of the ancients had been in the burial of their dead, giving a melodious turn of his own to each bit of dubious pedantry. He knew that burning and burying had gone hand in hand in all ages, and he does not confine himself to the Greeks and Romans. He took a vivid interest in ancient Scandinavian history, and knew something of the funeral rites of the Vikings. He actually quotes Danish, in this being perhaps unique among his English contemporaries, and he displays the surprising breadth of his accomplishment by showing familiarity, not once, nor twice, with the *Purgatorio* as well as the *Inferno* of Dante.

A learned German had preceded Browne in the serious part of his inquiry. In 1604, Johann Kirchmann of Lübeck (1575–1643) published at Hamburg a Latin work *De Funeribus Romanorum,* which enjoyed a great success, and in Browne's day continued to be the recognised authority on the subject. It is significant of the literary rather than scientific spirit in which these archæological themes were approached in the seventeenth century, that the *De Funeribus* consisted of a course of lectures which Kirchmann had delivered while he was professor of poetry at Rostock. Browne does not quote Kirchmann by name more than

two or three times; but it has been proved that he
borrowed his references very extensively from the
Rostock professor, whose book had not been translated
into English.   He is very glad to dwell on all evidences
of the burning of the body, and was deeply in sympathy with the purifying action of the flames, "refining
the grosser commixture and firing out the ethereal
particles so deeply immersed in" the earthly tissues
of the body.   It is evident that Sir Thomas Browne
would have heartily approved of the modern practice
of cremation.   He speaks with the greatest horror of
the fear which assails us of "being knaved out of
our graves," and of having "our skulls made into
drinking-bowls."

It is not less than extraordinary that the one great
English author who has expressed a definite terror of
having his bones tampered with and his skull exhibited, should be the one who has suffered from that
shocking outrage.   In 1840, some workmen who were
digging a grave for the wife of the incumbent of St.
Peter Mancroft, in Norwich, broke into the neighbour-
ing vault where the body of Sir Thomas Browne had
lain since 1682, and called the sexton to look at what
they had found.   The sexton saw below him the
skeleton of the great antiquary, and bending into the
tomb, seized the skull and carried it off.   He offered
it for sale, and it was bought by a collector over whose
name, in my opinion, it is best to shed the poppy of
oblivion.   This unworthy man, after amusing himself
with his sacrilegious possession, deposited it in a
museum in Norwich, "where it is still to be seen."
Mr. Charles Williams, the Norwich surgeon who has
done so much for the bibliography of Browne, stated

in 1897 that the skull had then " recently been claimed
by the Vicar of St. Peter Mancroft, but unsuccess-
fully "! I have seen no denial of this last statement,
which seems to imply an impious vulgarity almost
incredible.

Browne's solicitude with regard to the actual substance of the human body, and of separate parts of it,
after death, is almost grotesque. Certain ideas, as we
get to perceive as we become familiar with his writings, recurred very constantly to his thoughts. There
was an old legend that King Pyrrhus's toe could not be
burnt, and references to this privileged and immortal
member recur over and over in the works of Browne.
The incombustible toe has its paragraph in the chapter
on the Phœnix in the *Vulgar Errors* and is not over-
looked in that portion of the *Urn-Burial* which deals
with the burning of corpses. Browne even celebrated
this unlikely theme in verse, and the following epigram
occurs among his posthumous fragments : —

" O for a toe, such as the funeral pyre
   Could make no work on — proof 'gainst flame and fire ;
   Which lay unburnt when all the rest burnt out,
   Such amianthine toes might scorn the gout ;
   And the most flaming blast the gout could blow,
   But prove an *ignis fatuus* to that toe."

The most curious instance of this uncanny interest in
the animal part of humanity is, however, Browne's
pride in his discovery of a substance unknown to
science before his day, adipocere, or a wax of human
fat. In odd prowlings about the tombs of those long
dead he, in fact, observed for the first time a curious
fawn-coloured matter, unctuous and ductile, which was
the result of decomposition in damp places sheltered

from the air. The chemists say that it consists chiefly of ammonium margarate, with certain admixtures. At all events, the discovery of this substance was one of Browne's most prominent services to pure science, and we may fancy his imagination tracing the noble adipocere of Alexander until he found it stopping a hole to keep the wind away. He would certainly have scorned Horatio for holding that it was to consider too curiously to consider so. These were the light sides and easy reductions of the great and solemn mystery of death.

The spacious music of the *Urn-Burial,* from which we have allowed ourselves to turn for a moment, rises to its height in the paragraphs of the fifth chapter, over which the reader is fain to delay, since here it is unquestionable that he has the genius of Thomas Browne revealed to him in its fullest splendour. Here the author has done with antiquarian speculation, done with the various Italian and German authorities on whom he based his curious erudite technicality, and he turns to devote himself to the poetry of the situation. He contemplates once more, and with a deeper intensity, these poor bones from Walsingham that have "quietly rested under the drums and tramplings of three conquests"; and he contrasts the diuturnity of these frail remains, which never sought for anything but shelter and forgetfulness, with the oblivion which has attended the bones of great emperors who designed that their monuments should outlast the ages. He wonders, too, in what conditions those rustics came to die; whether it was disease or old age which carried them slowly to their graves, or whether they "died by violent hands, and were thrust into their urns," an alternative that would, he thinks, deepen the interest with which we contemplate them, as beings who descended with the fierce gust of life still brilliant in them, and not dulled and quenched by indistinct decline.   All these and many other problems vex him as he gazes into the little urns of clay, and he feels how bewildering and how vain it is, and yet how attractive and how irresistible, to speculate what manner of men and women and children these were, and what faint desires of re-union with their kind may have stirred their obscure souls : —

"What song the Syrens sang, or what name Achilles assumed when he hid himself among women, though puzzling questions, are not beyond all conjecture.   What time the persons of these ossuaries entered the famous nations of the dead, and slept with princes and counsellors, might admit a wide solution.   But who were the proprietaries of these bones, or what bodies these ashes made up, were a question above antiquarism ; not to be resolved by man, nor easily perhaps by spirits, except we consult the provincial guardians or tutelary observators.   Had they made as good provision for their names, as they have done for their relics, they had not so grossly erred in the art of perpetuation.   But to subsist in bones, and be but pyramidally extant, is a fallacy in duration.   Vain ashes, which in the oblivion of names, persons, times, and sexes, have found unto themselves a fruitless continuation, and only arise unto late posterity, as emblems of mortal vanities, antidotes against pride, vain-glory and madding vices.   Pagan vain-glories which thought the world might last for ever, had encouragement for ambition ; and, finding no Atropos unto the immortality of their names, were never dampt with the necessity of oblivion.   Even old ambitions had the advantage of ours, in the attempts of their vain-glories, who acting early, and before the probable meridian of time, have by this time found great accomplishment of their designs, whereby the ancient heroes have already outlasted

their monuments and mechanical preservations. But in this
latter scene of time, we cannot expect such mummies unto
our memories, when ambition may fear the prophecy of Elias
[that the world may last but six thousand years] and Charles
the Fifth can never hope to live within two Methuselahs of
Hector."

The remaining pages of the treatise are even more
ingeniously wrought and fuller of unusual music.
We shall return to them when we come to analyse the
peculiarities of the style of their author. When, however, we reach the last surprising paragraph, and turn
to a consideration of the whole rhapsody of *Urn-Burial*,
we shall probably say to ourselves that the radical
scepticism which was so vehemently denied in *Religio
Medici*, and again deprecated in the *Vulgar Errors*, has
here escaped into notice, unobserved by the author,
and can hardly any longer be refuted. It is true that
in the very final paragraph the desire to subsist in
lasting monuments, and to escape the universal pre-
dicament of oblivion, is mildly reproved. " All this,"
the judicious philosopher feels bound to remark, " is
nothing in the metaphysics of true belief." He
reminds himself, much as if a church bell had broken
in upon his studies, that he is not a priest of ancient
Syria but a respectable physician practising in the
Christian town of Norwich : —

" To live indeed is to be again ourselves, which being not
only an hope, but an evidence in noble believers, 'tis all one
to lie in St. Innocents' churchyard as in the sands of Egypt.
Ready to be anything, in the ecstasy of being ever, and as
content with six foot as the *molès* of Adrianus."

This is the only tribute to the Christian religion
which Browne's sombre treatise on the pomp of death

vouchsafes to give us. "Ready to be anything, in the ecstasy of being ever;" we must make what we may of this as an evidence of his attitude, at this period of his life, to the problems of faith and immortality.

The *Urn-Burial* was too short to be published by itself, and therefore there was added to it a treatise on which Browne, apparently at the same time, had been working. The dedicatory letter preceding *The Garden of Cyrus* is dated "May 1" (1658), as is that which presents the *Urn-Burial* to Thomas Le Gros of Crostwick. We must take this date, then, as being that on which the combined manuscripts were sent off to the printers, not that on which the composition of either of them was finished. It has been observed that the striking statement with which *The Garden of Cyrus* approaches its close, "the quincunx of heaven runs low," gives us a date, since the Hyades, the quincunx among the constellations, only approach the western horizon at midnight towards the beginning of March. It is curious that two of the three gentlemen who had originally invited Browne to take up his abode in Norwich in 1636, survived more than twenty years later to receive homage in the little volume which he published in his prime. Mr. Nicholas Bacon, of Gillingham, to whom *The Garden of Cyrus* was dedicated, was one of Browne's oldest and most intimate friends. He was the fourth son of Sir Edmund Bacon of Redgrave, second baronet, and became himself the first baronet of the Bacons of Gillingham. Sir Edmund Bacon of Redgrave, who died in 1649, had been intimately friendly with the physician, who appears to have attended all the branches of this

numerous and wealthy family. Nicholas Bacon had
been the consistent patron and intimate admirer of
Browne for more than thirty years, when he died in
1666. The Hall of Gillingham, with a park running
down to the north bank of the Waveney, was in the
extreme south of the county, almost on the borders
of Suffolk.

Browne had no " considerable garden " attached to
his house in Norwich. But Nicholas Bacon had
" wisely ordered his vegetable delights " at Gillingham,
and Browne was always a welcome and, we may be
sure, a garrulous visitor there. Bacon collected herbals;
he possessed even Besler's *Hortus Eystettensis,* the most
elephantine of a giant race; and no doubt it was in the
library at Gillingham that Browne culled some of his
most learned allusions. He was now eager, not only
for himself, but, as we shall presently see, for Evelyn,
to collect a nosegay of oddities out of the gardens of
the world. *The Garden of Cyrus,* to which we are
about to turn, is formidable enough in its present
congested state; we tremble to think what it might
have been, had Browne added those mathematical
truths which he was persuaded by Nicholas Bacon's
" discerning judgment" to omit. He scarcely permits
himself a rapture, yet cannot help ejaculating, as he
thinks of the flower-beds at Gillingham, " the Turks
who passed their days in gardens here, will have also
gardens hereafter, and delighting in flowers on earth,
must have lilies and roses in heaven." Perhaps
Nicholas Bacon was a little too fond of his borders,
and neglected his county duties for the sake of his
tulips, since Browne hints gently that " that insinuat-
ing pleasure is seldom without some extremity," and

adds, surprisingly, that "Cato seemed to dote upon cabbage." It is because of this amiable weakness in his friend, that the author of *The Garden of Cyrus* ventures to bring a somewhat fantastic treatise in the metaphysics of horticulture to present to the polite and learned squire of Gillingham, knowing him to be an intrepid gardener, and "a serious student in the highest arcana of nature."

The full title of Browne's most extraordinary, and, it must be confessed, most difficult literary production, is *The Garden of Cyrus, or, the Quincuncial, Lozenge or Net-Work Plantations of the Ancients, artificially, naturally, mystically considered.* A certain degree of attention is paid to the "botanical bravery" of "the Persian gallants," whose several very flowery attributes are celebrated in paragraphs which have no particular historical basis; but of Cyrus and his garden Browne has little enough information to give us. His name is simply borrowed to give a title to the tract because "all stories," our author declares, " do look upon Cyrus as the splendid and regular planter" of the quincunx. But what is a quincunx? This it is now a highly important point to decide, for we are entering a region thronged with specimens of this unfamiliar contrivance, an atmosphere which produced in the serious-minded S. T. Coleridge a sort of fit of hysterics, in which he declared that there were "quincunxes in heaven above, quincunxes in earth below, quincunxes in the mind of man, quincunxes in tones, in optic nerves, in roots of trees, in leaves, in everything."

The word "quincunx," for which Sir Thomas Browne cherished a love so extreme that he used it in and out of season as though magical virtue lodged in the very

sound of it, had not long before been introduced into
English use, by the astrologers of the school of William
Lilly, from whom Browne doubtless borrowed it.
Mr. W. A. Craigie defines a quincunx as an arrangement or disposition of five objects so placed that four
occupy the corners, and the fifth the centre of a square
or other rectangle. He considers that this sense is
due, in its original Latin signification, to the use of
five dots or dashes to denote five-twelfths of an as, and
he quotes Browne as the first English author to employ
it so. But the astrologers used the word to describe a
certain aspect of plants, and gardeners a certain arrangement of trees or plants in groups of five. "His
quincunx darkens, his espaliers meet," says Pope to
Lord Burlington, showing that Villario laid out part
of his plantations in sets of five trees each; and Peter-
borough helped the poet to do the same at Twickenham.
A massing of the quincunx arrangement produces an
effect analogous to that of the lines on a chess-board or
of lattice-work, while botanists recognise a quincuncial
structure in several of the parts of plants. This may
serve, perhaps, as enough to lighten with a glimmer
the porch of Browne's dark discourse.

It opens, indeed, with a sufficient illumination of its
own, in a charming claim for horticulture to take a
place above physic and surgery in our affections : —

"For though physic may plead high, from that medical
act of God, in casting so deep a sleep upon our first parent,
and surgery find its whole art in that one passage concerning
the rib of Adam; yet is there no rivality with garden contrivance and herbary. For, if Paradise were planted the
third day of the creation, as wiser divinity concludeth, the
nativity thereof was too early for horoscopy. Gardens were
before gardeners, and but some hours after the earth."

We then meander through the records of the ancients,
in the course of which, as we might have anticipated,
Browne does not fail to loiter, enamoured, in the
"pensile" or hanging gardens of Semiramis, or to
dwell on the cause of the humiliation of Nebuchad-
nezzar, whose "melancholy metamorphosis" he attributes to a re-action against his excess of satisfaction in
"the bravery of the paradise" of flowers which he had
built for himself overhanging his city of Babylon.
But all these reminiscences of antiquity soon concentrate on the contemplation of the quincunx pure and
simple, "the emphatical decussation or fundamental
figure" which Brown discovers in every record of
ancient gardening or plantation.   But, as though he
saw, down the avenue of time, the unborn Coleridge
waiting to laugh at his obsession, Browne gathers
himself together, and mentions several objects in
which he does *not* perceive the quincuncial arrangement.   He takes credit to himself, for instance, in dis-
missing the cross of St. Andrew, and the Labarum of
Constantine, and the Rabbinical Tenupha, and the
crux ansata on the bosom of Serapis, as none of them
necessarily quincuncial.   But having made this handsome concession, he seems to repent of it, and gathering
his forces together, during the remainder of *The Garden
of Cyrus* it is quincunx, quincunx all the way, till the
light of heaven seems darkened by this multitude of
revolving chess-boards.   The close of the first chapter,
into which we may gaze as into a dark and vitreous,
but translucent pool, offers a favourable example of the
strange jargon in which the whole treatise is composed.
It is all, perhaps, at first sight, unintelligible, but if we
keep our eyes fixed on the idea, not without some risk

of vertigo, we see the element to be pellucid, and we see Browne's fancies, like slow and aged fishes, gliding about in the twilight of it : —

"Since even in Paradise itself, the tree of knowledge was placed in the middle of the garden, whatever was the ambient figure, there wanted not a centre and rule of decussation. Whether the groves and sacred plantations of antiquity were not thus orderly placed, either by *quaternios,* or quintuple ordinations, may favourably be doubted. For since they were so methodical in the constitutions of their temples, as to observe the due situation, aspect, manner, form, and order in architectonical relations, whether they were not as distinct in their groves and plantations about them, in form and species respectively unto their deities, is not without probability of conjecture. And in their groves of the sun this was a fit number by multiplication to denote the days of the year ; and might hieroglyphically speak as much, as the mystical statue of Janus in the language of his fingers. And since they were so critical in the number of his horses, the strings of his harp, the rays about his head, denoting the orbs of heaven, the seasons and months of the year, witty idolatry would hardly be flat in other appropriations."

The second chapter of *The Garden of Cyrus* deals with the quincuncial form as adopted in the arts. We read of the mysterious arrangement in architecture, in painting, in sculpture, of " the ancient pillar-work observable in Ionic pieces " and of the " fasciations and handsome ligatures " fastened quincuncially about the heads of princes. It appears that the beds of the ancients were corded in a quincunx, and that the venerable game of knuckle-bones has its source in the same rhomboidal decussation. The nosegay-nets which, it seems, were suspended under the chins of kings, were eminently quincuncial, and so was the too-famous

network of Vulcan which, on a scandalous occasion,
caused inextinguishable laughter in heaven. Even the
"neat retiary spider," who spreads his glittering quincunx over the dewy furze-bushes at dawn, is not
forgotten, nor the pattern upon nutcrackers, nor the
Macedonian phalanx. Nothing is too noble, nothing
is too humdrum for Browne to drag it in. It would
almost have been simpler to have said that Providence
had arranged the entire universe in the form of a
chequer-board, and so have done with it. All is subdued to Browne's passion for remote, odd, and splendid
words; and if we are called upon to observe the quincuncial arrangement in "mascles, fusils, and saltyres,"
we may depend upon it that it is to give the author
an opportunity of employing terms so quaint and
rare.

He comes back to gardens, and the botanical world,
where indeed his contention has a considerable plausibility. He shows himself a careful scholar of the
herbalists of his day, and is closely, and picturesquely,
observant of the native plants of the county of Norfolk.
All this part of *The Garden of Cyrus*, however, is almost unreadable, so crabbed is it and so congested
with technical description of the " elegant co-ordina-
tion of vegetables." A burst of pure melodious fancy,
therefore, such as the following, trembling indeed
on the borderland of astrology, is highly refreshing
to the ear : —

" Could we satisfy ourselves in the position of the lights
above, or discover the wisdom of that order so invariably
maintained in the fixed stars of heaven ; could we have any
light, why the stellary part of the first mass separated into
this order, that the girdle of Orion should ever maintain its

line, and the two stars in Charles' wain never leave pointing at
the pole star ; we might abate the Pythagorical music of the
spheres, the sevenfold pipe of Pan, and the strange crypto-
graphy of Gaffarel in his starry book of heaven."

In his most serious consideration of natural objects
Browne flashes the dark lantern of his wit upon us,
often leaving us more dazzled than illuminated.
When, for instance, he is describing the bristling and
" palisadoed " head of that strange plant, the teazel,
he breaks off to remark, in his dreamy way, that
" in the house of the solitary maggot we may find
the seraglio of Solomon," immediately appending to
this harmonious, if mysterious, utterance, a string of
phrases so harsh and filled with words so ugly and
pedantic, that the teazel is a bush of velvet by the
side of them. It is certainly in *The Garden of Cyrus*
that we find Browne in his most provoking mood,
least attentive to the just requirements of literature,
and bent most wilfully in pandering to mere intellectual vanity, yet this radically bad book contains
some of the most lovely paragraphs which passed from
an English pen during the seventeenth century. Of
these the most famous is that with which the treatise
closes. The disquisition becomes particularly dull in
the final chapter, wandering away in the most tedious
fashion to astrological nonsense of all kinds, " nauseat-
ing crambe verities and questions over-queried." At
last it would seem that Browne put the exhausted
manuscript by, leaving it without an ending. Then,
inspired by precisely the same imaginative ecstasy in
which he composed the *Urn-Burial*, he turned to the
unfinished *Garden of Cyrus* on that midnight of March
1658, and rounded it off with a glorious final page.

We speak of purple passages, but was one more radiant than this ever woven upon the richest of Tyrian looms ?

"But the quincunx of Heaven runs low, and 'tis time to close the five ports of knowledge. We are unwilling to spin out our awaking thoughts into the phantasms of sleep, which often continueth precogitations, making cables of cobwebs and wildernesses of handsome groves. Besides, Hippocrates hath spoke so little, and the oneirocritical masters have left such frigid interpretations from plants, that there is little encouragement to dream of Paradise itself. Nor will the sweetest delight of gardens afford much comfort in sleep, wherein the dulness of that sense shakes hands with delectable odours, and, though in the bed of Cleopatra, can hardly with any delight raise up the ghost of a rose.

"Night, which Pagan theology could make the daughter of Chaos, affords no advantage to the description of order; although no lower than that mass can we derive its genealogy. All things began in order, so shall they end, and so shall they begin again; according to the ordainer of order and mystical mathematics of the city of heaven.

"Though Somnus in Homer be sent to rouse up Agamemnon, I find no such effects in these drowsy approaches of sleep. To keep our eyes open longer, were but to act our Antipodes. The huntsmen are up in America, and they are already past their first sleep in Persia. But who can be drowsy at that hour which freed us from everlasting sleep? Or have slumbering thoughts at that time, when sleep itself must end, and, as some conjecture, all shall awake again?"

The two treatises were published in one volume, in London, in 1658. The book contained, as its frontispiece, pictures of four of the Walsingham urns, drawn, as we are told, with a piece of charcoal found in one of them, and provided with a quincuncial tag out of Propertius. In front of *The Garden of Cyrus* was a print of the ground-plan of a network plantation.

K

In the month of January, in this fullest year of
Browne's intellectual existence, a further stimulus had
been given to his mental energy by a correspondence
with the celebrated John Evelyn. The philosopher
of Sayes Court had long harboured the idea of writing
a great book on gardens, which should swallow up all
the recognised herbals of the day, such as those of
Parkinson and Gerard, while treating horticulture on
a more purely scientific basis. This scheme was to
take the form of a huge *Elysium Britannicum*, but
although Evelyn continued to play with the notion
almost to the end of his life, the *magnum opus* never
appeared. What did, however, appear in this year,
1658, was Evelyn's graceful little book named the
French Gardiner, for which Browne's desultory help
was called in. By what Evelyn describes as "an extraordinary humanity" on Browne's part, the Norwich
physician threw himself warmly into Evelyn's plan;
and possibly too warmly, for his learning and sugges-
tions may have overpowered the spirits of the accomplished amateur, who was not accustomed to apply
himself to his themes with the vehement weight which
Browne brought to them. One human point which is
very curious is, that Evelyn's long letter to Browne on
the subject of "caves, grots, mounts, and irregular
ornaments of gardens" is dated January 28, 1658, and
was therefore written on the very day after the death
of his only son (January 27), the occasion when Evelyn
burst forth with "Here ends the joy of my life, and
for which I go ever mourning to the grave." His
anguish at the loss of this exquisite child — "for
beauty of body, a very angel; for endowment of mind,
of incredible and rare hopes" — was poignant and

permanent. The stoicism, therefore, which writes at
such length, on a scientific matter, to a fellow-
philosopher, with the little tender body hardly laid
out in the room above, is remarkable for its dignity.
Yet, before Evelyn can close his epistle, a cry of nature
breaks forth.

Browne, although already busy upon his *Urn-
Burial*, responded warmly to Evelyn's appeal, and
indeed the letter to which reference has just been
made acknowledges the receipt of " papers which you
have transmitted me."   In the preface to his *Acetaria*,
published more than forty years later, Evelyn described
what his plan had been of a vast work on a royal
garden. It appears that Browne was to undertake
several sections in the book, and the names of these
are fitted to stimulate our curiosity.   There was to
be a chapter by Browne " Of Garden Burial," another
" Of Stupendous and Wonderful Plants," another " Of
Paradise and of the most famous Gardens in the world."
One section, " Of the Coronary Garden," survives, and
unquestionably belongs to this year of Browne's climac-
teric, 1658. It is a charming specimen of his richest
prose. The " use of flowery crowns and garlands "
excites our philosopher to the height of his mellifluity,
and he revels in fragrant and floral imagery. A
passage from this essay may be compared with what
we find in its better-known cœvals, the *Urn-Burial*
and the *Garden of Cyrus* : —

" In their convivial gardens [the ancient Greeks] had respect
unto plants preventing drunkenness, or discussing [*i.e.* dispers-
ing] the exhalations of wine ; wherein, besides roses, taking
in ivy, vervain, and melilote, they made use of divers of small
beauty or good odour. The solemn festival garlands were

made properly unto their gods, and accordingly contrived
from the plants sacred unto such deities; and their sacrificial
ones were selected under such circumstances. Their honorary
crowns triumphal, ovary, civical, obsidional, had little of
flowers in them; and their funeral garlands had little of
beauty in them besides roses, while they made them of myrtle,
rosemary, and *apium*, under symbolical intimations. But our
florid and purely ornamental gardens, delightful unto sight
and smell, nor framed according to any mystical and symbolical considerations, are of more free election, and so may
be made to excel those of the ancients. We have China,
India, and a New World to supply us, besides the great distinction of flowers unknown unto antiquity, and the varieties
thereof arising from art and nature."

There can be little doubt that the long posthumous
tract, called *Observations upon several Plants mentioned
in Scripture*, was also composed at this time as a contribution to Evelyn's projected *Elysium*. According to a
pencil note in Evelyn's handwriting, the *Observations*
would seem to have been addressed in the form of letters "to Sir Nicholas Bacon." Evelyn doubtless meant
Mr. Nicholas Bacon of Gillingham, to whom, as we
have seen, the *Garden of Cyrus* was dedicated. It may
be conjectured, indeed, that that work also was composed as a chapter of the great book on gardens, and
was perhaps published in 1658, because Evelyn may
have sent it back to its author as being admirable in
itself, but not fitted to his particular design. We may
further observe that Tenison, writing in 1686, shortly
after Browne's death, speaks of having selected the
plant chapters above mentioned "out of many disordered papers," so that Browne's contributions to the
imaginative treatment of horticulture were probably
much more extensive than those which we now possess.

Doubtless, also, the reason why he did not, during his own lifetime, publish these highly-characteristic portions of his work was that he was always waiting for Evelyn to complete his design — a design which was not finally abandoned until 1699.

In the letter which accompanied the manuscript of his essay, "On the Coronary Garden," Browne announced another on the incision and propagation of plants, that is to say, on grafting. This occurs among the papers first printed by Simon Wilkin in 1835, and the very long catalogue of proposed experiments which it includes shows what an ardent gardener Browne had now become. Norwich was famous for its gardens and orchards, "very much addicted," as Evelyn puts it, "to the flowery part." Browne either had made, or intended shortly to make, an incredible number of graftings, such as of a hornbeam upon a beech, a maple upon a hornbeam, a sycamore upon a maple, ringing the changes upon all possible trees, and even such, one would suppose, hopeless experiments on bushes as grafting rosemary upon ivy, and a gooseberry on a mezereon. In the meadows around Norwich he had observed currants and berberries growing on the pollard heads of willows, and this suggested to him a garden which should be a sort of museum of complicated botanical "freaks." All this throws amusing light on his eagerness and even his credulity, although he believed himself exceedingly clear-sighted. When Evelyn, for instance, talked loosely about miraculous gardens seen floating about, masses of ambulatory blossom on the backs of huge fishes, Browne, with grave courtesy, suggested a sceptical attitude towards this "rather extraordinary and anomalous" phenomenon.

It would seem that Browne's correspondence with
Evelyn soon came to a close, and it is very noticeable
that when, a year or two later, Evelyn was looking
about for men of high scientific attainment to form a
sort of first committee of the Royal Society, his choice
does not seem to have fallen upon his brilliant and
learned acquaintance at Norwich. I do not know that
any conjecture has been made as to the reason of
Browne's exclusion from, or at least non-inclusion in,
that interesting body. I would suggest as a plausible
cause the reputation which Browne had now gained as
an infatuated astrologer. We have to take into full
consideration the hold which the chimerical art had
taken on the minds of learned men of his generation.
The sixteenth century had reeked of geomancy and
divination; they had tainted all the physical science of
that age. In the earliest times, Galen had encouraged
medical astrology; he accepted, he perhaps first de-
fined, the morbific influence of the moon. Paracelsus,
though sceptical, had admitted the existence of astral
diseases, and Cardan, a consistent necromancer, is said
to have starved himself rather than that the predicted
date of his death should pass and he survive. These
were names, and these were traditions, which weighed
on the minds of physicians of the class of Browne, who
firmly believed that the therapeutic action of different
metals corresponded to the influence of each planet, so
that Venus, a type benevolent and mild, was the equi-
valent of copper, while the morose and sinister Saturn
was represented by lead. The pathological influence
of stars was firmly believed in, and survived among
leading physicians until the beginning of the eighteenth
century, when it is extraordinary to find such an

enlightened man as Richard Mead still acknowledging the possibility of a lunar influence in medicine.

It is curious that experience and common sense did not intervene to destroy this maddest of vulgar errors.[1] But the aspect of the planets particularly in the prevalence of mysterious epidemics, and in the deaths of kings, was not to be put by. It was Voltaire, when he riddled the whole empirical art of divination with his wit, who may be said to have given astrology its death-blow. He it was who pointed out the snobbishness of the stars, which attended only to the fates of popes and princes; " il n'y avait d'étoiles que pour eux: le reste de l'univers était de la canaille dont les étoiles ne se mêlaient pas." Browne, from the nature of his imagination, from his tendency to the mysterious and the transcendental part of thought, was the easy prey of the astrologers. He had become intimate with Arthur Dee, a doctor in practice at his side in the parish of St. George Tomblands, in Norwich, who was a son of the yet more notorious necromancer, Dr. John Dee. Arthur Dee thrilled Browne with accounts of how he was initiated into the use of the magic stone, a globe of polished quartz crystal, with which his father did tremendous things in the castle of Tribau in Bohemia.

[1] We may note that mere erudition rather fostered it. Mark Pattison points out that the most learned man in Europe in the previous generation, Isaac Casaubon, swallowed all the astounding fictions of alchemy. " All belief is with him a question of authority and books; if a great author has said a thing it is so." What was necessary for the new philosophy to do was to insist, as Descartes did, that sense was not the monopoly of the book-learned, who, as a matter of fact, were blinded by their superstitious respect for the ancients.

In 1651, Arthur Dee had died in Norwich, after, it would seem, introducing Browne to a more remarkable man, and a still more ardent astrologer. When he was resident in Moscow, twenty years before his death, Arthur Dee composed in Latin a highly recondite *Arcanum of Hermetic Philosophy*, which no less a person than Elias Ashmole translated, concealing his own name under an anagram. Dee seems to have been the link which united the inner circle of English astrologers together, Ashmole, and Lilly, and Booker and Backhouse. In 1653, the dying Backhouse had whispered to Ashmole, syllable by syllable, the true and innermost secret of the Philosopher's Stone; this would have been a more impressive event, if Backhouse had not come to life again for nine more years, and if Ashmole had not meanwhile forgotten the formula.

In this circle of mystery, there is evidence that Browne desired to tread. He was the depositary of Arthur Dee's manuscripts, and in 1658 he offered to lend them to Ashmole, "but I shall intreat the favour to have them returned." He repeated to Ashmole, in perfect gravity, monstrous stories of alchemy and geomancy with which Arthur Dee had gulled him, or had himself been gulled. It is true that during the Commonwealth there was a great recrudescence of astrological superstition in western Europe, and that England did not escape. No doubt, within the new-born Royal Society itself, there were many who believed in the malefic aspect of the stars, and dreamed of the philosopher's stone. But they did not publish their faith, and the whole tendency of the society was to discourage the condition of mind in which a belief in the chimerical formulas of the astrologers was possible. If

we are surprised to find that Thomas Browne was
neither an original nor an elected member of the
Royal Society, it is surely enough to recollect that he
was known too well as the author of *The Garden of
Cyrus*.

Towards the autumn of the eventful year 1658,
Browne received a letter from Mr. (afterwards Sir
William) Dugdale, the already celebrated antiquary
and herald, whom he had quoted by name in the
Urn-Burial. Dugdale, emboldened by this civility to
believe himself known to the Norwich naturalist,
ventured, although a stranger, to address a letter of
inquiry to Browne. This was met by Browne with
his accustomed effusive courtesy, and already in
October he is Dugdale's "much-honoured friend."
Dugdale had, in the preceding year, made a tour
through the fen-country at the desire of Lord Gorges,
who was surveyor-general of the Great Level, and
who commissioned Dugdale to write a book, which
appeared at last, in 1662, as the *History of Imbanking
and Draining of divers Fens and Marshes*. The herald
had some inquiries to make of Browne respecting the
natural history of that district, and in particular with
regard to a curious fossil fish, found on Conington
Down, near Soham. Dugdale, on his part, is desired
to give Browne information about urns and Roman
coins which have turned up in these explorations of
the Fens, and the antiquary is vexed at being unable
to gratify his friend by adding to Browne's numis-
matical collections. When Dugdale, who wrote first
from his country house, Blyth Hall in Warwickshire,
returns to London, he is laid up for several weeks
with the scurvy, when Elias Ashmole takes up the

correspondence with Browne for him, until Dugdale is well again in the spring of 1659. He is busy, meanwhile, on the second volume of his famous *Monasticon*, and applies for all manner of information to Browne, who gossips to him in return about rare birds he has been seeing in the fields, and strange seaweeds he has been picking up on the shore of Norfolk.

CHAPTER V

LAST YEARS: 1659–1682

No one observed the dying flutter of the Commonwealth with more eagerness, or welcomed the return of royalty with greater joy than Thomas Browne. On Coronation Day, his calm spirit was quite unusually exalted, and his description of the great doings in Norwich is jubilant. He notes with exultation that Cromwell is being hanged and burned in effigy everywhere; and he grimly adds, "whose head is now upon Westminster Hall, together with Ireton's and Bradshaw's." Norwich broke out into beacon bonfires; there were feasts here and feasts there, one little play was acted by strollers in the Market Place, and another by young citizens on a stage at Timber Hill. There was no resistance to the king in Norwich, where "it is thought by degrees most will come to conformity"; nor to the Church, for the observation of Lent is reinstituted, which "makes Yarmouth and fishermen rejoice." Dr. Browne moves up and down the streets of the city, exulting in the happy change, and greeting one highly respectable client after another with that "civil and debonair" expansiveness for which he was famous, while the great minster bells of Christ Church peal forth in the early April morning, and can scarcely be persuaded to cease until the stroke of noon.

On the 17th of August 1661, in consequence of these great affairs, Edward Reynolds, who had been consecrated Bishop of Norwich, came to take up his residence at the Palace, which had been deserted since the Puritans turned out Joseph Hall. Reynolds, a very liberal churchman, who had been Warden of Merton College, Oxford, was the "loving friend" of Browne, and his arrival a great delight to the philosopher, who was careful in his attendance at the Cathedral when the bishop preached, with his croaking voice, but eloquently, on the 25th of August. It is interesting to note, as an instance of the long hunger of the Anglican worshippers now satisfied at last, that Browne records the delight he feels at seeing Reynolds in his place at church. "He sitteth," he says gleefully, "in his seat against the pulpit, handsomely built up and in his episcopal vestments, and pronounceth the Blessing or the Peace of God at the end." It was long since Christ Church Cathedral had seen such seemly ritual.

The education of a remarkably fine and intelligent brood of children occupied Dr. Thomas and Mrs. Dorothy Browne very pleasantly and fully at this period of their lives. The domestic records of the family are charming to an unusual degree. The young people were trained carefully and firmly, without severity, and it is to be specially noticed that the father spared to each of them a degree of sympathetic consideration which was rare indeed in those days of stiff parental rigour. To his sons, at a very tender age, we find Thomas Browne writing as to valued friends, anxious to share his interests with them, studiously careful not to wound their susceptibilities or to hold them at a distance. He was rewarded by a touching devotion and, from those who survived him, by an almost adoring piety. Bread cast upon the waters never came back to the giver more plenteously than did Browne's loving solicitude for his children. It is time that we should be introduced to these young persons, although it is a little difficult to be sure that we can count them all. One infant daughter, Dorothy, had died in 1652; two other daughters, Elizabeth, afterwards Mrs. Lyttleton, and Anne, afterwards Mrs. Fairfax, are patent to us as born about 1648 and 1650. A fourth daughter, Lady Cotterell, cannot be clearly placed; but the two sons, delightful boys, and the apples of their father's eyes, are plain enough.

Edward, the eldest of the family, and certainly the most gifted, was born at Norwich in 1644, and was therefore a lad of sixteen at the time of the Restoration. He was succeeded, in 1646, by Thomas, who inherited a less buoyant constitution, with some melancholy in his temperament, but was eminently " biddable" and trustworthy. Both boys received their earliest training in the Norwich grammar school, and Edward went, in 1659, to Trinity College, Cambridge. It seems to have been thought that "honest Tom" was more fitted for business, and therefore in the autumn of 1660, although only fourteen years of age, he was sent alone, in a vintage ship, from Yarmouth to Bordeaux, apparently that he might learn French and study the wine trade. The tender and anxious letters which his parents wrote to him have been preserved, and are very pleasant reading. Except that he had introductions to a Mr. Dade in Bordeaux, and was well supplied with money from home, the boy, who knew no French, seems to have been thrown entirely on his own resources. He did not stay long in Bordeaux; we find him at Saintes, at La Rochelle, at Cognac, at the island of Rhé. His father's advices to him are what we should expect them to be:—

"Be not dejected and melancholy because you can yet have little comfort in conversation, and all things will seem strange unto you. Remember the camel's back, and be not troubled for anything that, otherwise, would trouble your patience here. Be courteous and civil to all; put on a decent boldness, and avoid *pudor rusticus*, not much known in France. Hold firm to the Protestant Religion, and be diligent in going to church when you have any little knowledge of the language. . . . View and understand all notable buildings and places in Bordeaux or near it, and take a draught thereof, as also the ruined Amphitheatre, but these at your leisure."

This was at "honest Tom's" first start, but he soon grew proficient in the French language and customs. He seems to have lived the longest part of his time with an apothecary in Saintes. His father was anxious lest his youth should lead him to take too much violent exercise; "be temperate," he says, "and stir little in the hot season." His parents were anxious he should be happy, and they pressed him to take lessons in singing and dancing, at their expense. But the poor boy was home-sick for Norwich, and we find him the victim of a settled "mallencholy," for which it seemed to him that the air of Norfolk should be prescribed. Discipline, however, must be maintained, and Tom had to wear out his year, and more

than a year, among the alien French. His father
advises, as a cure for his low spirits, that he should
"learn handsome songs and airs, not by book, but by
the ear as you shall hear them sung." But the best
music for "honest Tom" seems to have been the
announcement, which came at last, in March 1662,
that he might pack up his boxes and come home by
Nantes and Paris. On the 27th of April, "we came
unto the great city, and, as the French will have it,
the little world of Paris," says the boy in the very
intelligent and lucid journal which he kept for his
anxious parents' entertainment.

Edward, now B.A. of Trinity, was doing well at
Cambridge, and in September of the year in which
Tom came back from France, the parents allowed the
brothers to take a trip together for pleasure into
Derbyshire. They wrote a capital account of their
adventures, their father being solicitous that they
should early practise to write, so as to have "a good
pen and style." Here is a little touch in their journal
that is picturesque in itself, and valuable as showing
that their home was loved by them both. After a
delightful fortnight, closely packed with pleasures,

"to consumate all, that famous spire of Norwich presents
itself to our view, Christ Church high spire, the old famous
castle, eight and thirty goodly churches, the fields about it
and the stately gardens in it, did so lessen our opinion of any
[other place] we had seen, that it seemed to deride our ramb-
ling folly, and forced a new admiration from us of those things
which, with their often view had dulled our conceptions and
due estimation of their worth. . . . Let any stranger find me
out so pleasant a county, such good ways, large heath, three
such places as Norwich, Yar., and Lynn, in any county of
England, and I'll be once again a vagabond to visit them."

Tom, in spite of the French business, went back to Cambridge with Edward, and in July 1663 we find their father congratulating both on their advance in their studies, though with a playful grimace about the cost, "they have proved very chargeable." It was by this time fixed that Edward should be a doctor, and he took his decree of bachelor of physic at Cambridge. Being nineteen years of age, he now came back to Norwich to continue his studies under his father's eye. From New Year's Day 1664 the young *medicus* kept a diary of his doings, part doubtless of his father's careful plan for training him to be a man of letters like himself; it is preserved for a great part of the year, and it enables us to get several glimpses of the home life in the Browne household, until in February the young gentleman, tired of so much dancing by night and dissecting by day, rides up to London to study at Surgeons' Hall, where he is handsomely entertained, doubtless for his father's sake, by the eminent Dr. Windet. A daughter of Browne's, whose Christian name seems to be lost, had by this time married Sir Charles Cotterell, and Edward is made much of at his sister's "house in St. James' Park, handsomely built on a piece of ground, which the king gave to Sir Charles." In March, after riding all night "through that pleasant county of Essex," Edward is back at Norwich, and resumes his former course of life, dancing, dissecting, going to church, and prescribing for his father's patients; and in April starting for France, on the medical grand tour, just as his father had done more than thirty years before.

In agreement with the kindly practice of the family, Edward begins even before he sets foot in Calais to

write to his people at home. If this were the biography of Edward Browne and not of his father, his
delightful letters, full of ardour and keen observation,
excellently written, too, with a flowing pen, and not
with the habitual pedantic stick of the travelling
student of that age, would enrich the narrative with
an abundance of touches. We can only dwell on the
kindliness of the boy who supplies to his father exactly
the medical and antiquarian gossip which he knows he
will enjoy. And throughout his travels, Edward is
staunch in his devotion to home; "I prefer our little
garden at Norwich before that of Luxembourg in
Paris." The really exciting news is that he meets
with old Guy Patin, who welcomed *Religio Medici* so
many years before, and he must give his father all the
account of him he can. But Browne, for some reason,
required the services of his eldest son at home, and a
letter telling Edward that he cannot be spared any
later than Michaelmas puts the lad "into doleful dumps,
and spoils all the fine chimeras and geographical ideas
that I had formed in my brain of seeing Spain, Italy,
Germany, and I cannot tell how many countries."
But this was only postponed, for Edward Browne was
destined to be one of the great travellers of his age.
Even now, he overpersuaded the indulgence at home,
and got leave in October, instead of coming back to
Norwich, to pass down into Italy and spend the
winter in Rome, Naples, and Venice. He did not find
his way back to Norwich, indeed, until the autumn of
1665, when he firmly promises, in return for so much
indulgence, to spend a great deal of his time — all the
winter — in distilling and dissecting for his father.
His last act in Paris was to try to arrange for a French

L

translation of the *Vulgar Errors* to be undertaken by
a M. Pierre Briot. Thomas Browne was interested in
this, and sent Edward copies of the third and fourth
editions of the book, but nothing came of it.

At least as early as 1651, and while he was engaged
in writing the *Vulgar Errors*, Browne had come into
communication, one has a difficulty in surmising how,
with an Icelandic naturalist, Theodor Jónsson (Theodorus Jonas), who was minister of the parish of
Hitterdal. It appears that every year, at that time,
a vessel passed between Iceland and Yarmouth, and
when once Browne had established relations with his
northern friend, punctual correspondence, in Latin,
was carried on between them, for more than twenty
years. Browne's letters are lost; they may possibly
lurk in the drawers of a smoke-dried cabinet in some
remote Icelandic parsonage, but some of those written
by Jónsson remain, and testify to Browne's curiosity
and his friend's eagerness to gratify it. In 1663, from
particulars supplied him by Jónsson, Browne drew up
an *Account of Island, alias Iceland*, for the Royal
Society, in the course of which he speaks of his "long
acquaintance" with inhabitants of that then so remote and mysterious country. We learn from Edward
Browne's diary that in February 1664, the Brownes
had a visit in Norwich from "the Bishop's son of
Skalhault in Islande," from whom they heard "many
things concerning his country." The Bishop of
Skalholt at that time was Brynjolf Gizursson, one
of the most learned Icelanders of his age, to whose
magnificent collection of books and manuscripts later
scholarship owes a great debt. It is very interesting
to find Browne in communication with the cloistered

intellectual life of Iceland, then keeping its flame alive in an almost total isolation. The centre of that life, in the seventeenth century, was Skalholt.[1]

It is with the greatest regret that Thomas Browne's biographer is now forced to chronicle the most culpable and the most stupid action of his life. In doing so, we can offer ourselves no other consolation than to say that his head and not his heart must have been at fault. By a curious irony, it was not until he had just passed away, in honoured old age, that this blot on Browne's record was made generally public, in an appendix to some posthumous tracts of Sir Matthew Hale, printed in 1683. That strong, harsh judge had condemned two unhappy women to death for witch-craft at the Bury St. Edmunds assizes on the 1st of March 1664. Among the appalling stories of witch-trials, none was more shocking, none more inexcusable than that which resulted in the hanging of Amy Duny and Rose Cullender. They were accused, on thirteen

---

[1] To the kindness of Sir Archibald Geikie I am indebted for the proof that this connection with Iceland was kept up by Thomas Browne much longer than has hitherto been known. Among the manuscript correspondence in the archives of the Royal Society, there exists a letter from Edward Browne to the Secretary, Dr. Henry Oldenburg, in which he says : " My father having divers years sent into Iceland, and received at several times some natural curiosities and answers to his inquiries from a learned divine there, Theodorus Jonas — one of what letters was formerly [in 1663] communicated to the R. S. by the hands of Sir Samuel Tuke — this year was brought him" some specimens of lava and a lump of sulphur from Mount Hekla, which Edward Browne forwards for inspection. The letter is undated, but Oldenburg has docketed it "Recd. October 10, 1673." The original manuscript of Thomas Browne's communication of 1663, published in the *Posthumous Works*, has not been preserved in the Royal Society.

counts, of practising sorcery to the hurt of the children
of their neighbours. The whole thing, patently, was
a piece of village malice ; it was traced back to a sordid
quarrel about some herrings. But a wretched woman,
proved to be of the worst character, swore that she
had long suspected Rose Cullender of being a witch,
and so had hung up her child's blanket in the chimney.
In the morning there was a toad in the blanket, which
she, standing beside the witch, threw into the fire,
whereupon it " made a great and horrible noise, and
flashed like gunpowder, and went off like a pistol, and
then became invisible, and by this [Rose Cullender]
was scorched and burnt lamentably."

For this monstrous tale the witness produced no
support, but it was taken with the evidence of children
who had had fits, and, in particular, of one little girl
who produced a glib tale of taps and touches, and
pricks with pins, but whose testimony was rejected by
the very prosecution. Sir Matthew Hale, though an
unflinching judge, was in this case extremely dubious ;
he was impressed by the utter worthlessness of the
witnesses and of their flimsy story. Unhappily,
Dr. Thomas Browne, " the famous physician of his
time," was in court. Some of Browne's own friends,
such as Lord Cornwallis and Sir Edmund Bacon, with
the eminent lawyer, Serjeant Keeling, had expressed
their belief that the charges against the two women
were " a mere imposture." The Lord Chief Baron, in
his perplexity, turned to Browne as his last resource,
and asked him " to give his judgment in the case."
The court was against the prosecution ; a word in their
favour, or silence alone, would have saved the lives of
the miserable women. At this solemn juncture Browne

" declared, that he was clearly of opinion that the fits were natural, but heightened by the Devil, co-operating with the malice of the witches, at whose instance he did the villanies." He added that "in Denmark there had been lately a great discovery of witches, who used the very same way of afflicting persons, by conveying pins into them, and crooked, as these pins were, with needles and nails." He solemnly explained his opinion to be that the devil had co-operated with the " malice " of Amy Duny and Rose Cullender to stir up and excite the humours of the children's bodies so as to bring on distempers to which they were constitutionally subject, heightening these natural diseases "to a great excess by his subtilty." Whether he ultimately had, or had not, a scruple in his mind as to the wisdom of his judicial opinion, we cannot surmise. But he made a curious entry in his *Commonplace Book* : "We are no way doubtful that there are witches, but have not been always satisfied in the application of their witchcrafts." It is probable that in his remarks about Denmark, on which he laid much stress, Browne was referring to a famous witch-trial which had taken place at Kjöge, in Zealand, in 1662, when four miserable women had been burned alive.

Browne's declaration influenced the jury against mercy. We are told that " it turned back the scale, that was otherwise inclining to the favour of the accused persons." The judge still hesitated, but " put it off from himself as much as he could," resting on Browne's opinion. Still troubled in his conscience, Sir Matthew Hale finally left it to the jury, praying "that the great God of Heaven would direct their hearts in that weighty matter "; but it was the opinion

of the great doctor of Norwich that weighed with
them. They brought in Rose Cullender and Amy
Duny guilty upon all the thirteen several indictments.
They were hanged at Bury, protesting their innocence,
and their blood, poor creatures, was on the head of
the author of *Religio Medici*. With the exception of
the three Exeter witches who were executed in 1682,
these were perhaps the last persons hanged for witch-
craft in England. The case was the subject of protest
almost from the first, and was much used by those who
bravely attacked this judicial frenzy. It is observable
that the Rev. Francis Hutchinson, the first of those
who openly and courageously denounced witch-trials
as one of "the worst corruptions of religion and the
greatest perversions of justice," was a child at Bury
St. Edmunds when this ghastly crime was committed.

In June 1665 Browne had a curious experience.
His house in St. Peter's stood higher than any of its
neighbours, and was therefore exposed to the elements.
During a terrific thunder-storm which broke over
Norwich, he, "with many others, saw fire-balls fly
and go off when they met with resistance." One of
these fire-balls carried away the tiles and boards of
the little wooden pinnacle of a "leucomb"[1] window
in the doctor's house, breaking against it with a report
like that of two or three cannons. A curiously similar

---

[1] This word is not in Dr. Murray's *Oxford Dictionary*, and
he can offer me no elucidation of its meaning. Mr. Austin
Dobson, however, proposes to me a solution which is very
ingenious, and, I think, almost certainly right. He suggests
that it must be a corruption of the French word *lucarne*, an
opening in the roof of a house to light up the loft or garret.
Browne uses it several times, spelling it "leucome" as well
as "leucomb."

phenomenon had occurred in 1656, when the storm of
"fire-balls" was succeeded by hail that broke £3000
worth of glass in Norwich.   On each occasion the
pranks played by the *ignis fulmineus* were fantastic
and considerable, but "all this, God be thanked!
without mischief unto any person."

While Edward Browne was abroad, and was writing
home to his father his extremely full and interesting
impressions of what he saw, Tom, the second son, was
hastily distracted from his Cambridge studies by the
breaking out of the Dutch War. He was now eighteen
years of age, and he determined to go up to London
and secure a commission in the Navy. He seems,
from a phrase in one of his father's letters of November
1664, to have taken this step very abruptly; Browne,
not objecting, but full of paternal anxiety, writes to
him to "do nothing rashly but as you find just grounds
for your advantage, which will hardly be, at the best
deservings, without good and faithful friends.   No
sudden advantage for raw, though dangerous, services.
God and good friends advise you.   Be sober and com-
placent.   If you could quit periwigs it would be better
and more for your credit."   He suggests that Tom
might be learning Latin at his odd moments, which,
as advice for a hot lad, with one foot at sea and one on
shore, seems a little excessive. Mrs. Browne, ever the
worst of spellers, forwards in haste a "buf cotte" to
Tom by the "choch," and entreats him to "bee suer
to spand" as few "monyes" as he can.   Both parents
are all in a flutter over this bold duckling who has
taken so suddenly to the water, but "I besich God
bles and dereckt you," says loving Dorothy Browne.
Honest Tom had no difficulty in getting his com-

mission; and on the 21st of December arrived at
Portsmouth, and attached himself to the fleet of
Admiral Sir Jeremiah Smith. It was not until the
6th of January 1665 that he set sail from Spithead,
with a last agitated postscript from his father to be
sure and not forget to wear flannel next his skin.
Those at home "pray for their pretty brother daily."

Fragments of Tom Browne's log are extant, and
offer a very interesting record of a young officer's
experience on board a battle-ship in war time. His
vessel was the *Mountague*, a ship of the third class,
which accompanied the rest of the fleet to Spain, and
anchored off Cadiz, watching for the enemy. He was
transferred to the *Foresight*, and passed up the Mediterranean. In September 1665 he distinguished himself
in the Earl of Sandwich's capture of the Dutch fleets
at Bergen, in Norway, and took part in all the battles
of 1666. In May 1667, on board the *Marie Rose*, he
formed part of the convoy which conducted thirty-
eight merchant-vessels up to Plymouth Sound. He
was now a lieutenant, and his record had been an
admirable one. Although he was but twenty-one
years of age, he was officially described as "a sober,
studious, courageous, and diligent person," and no one
in all the fleet was like him, "so civil, observing, and
diligent to his charge, with the reputation and love
of all the ship." Those who wrote home made his
father's heart swell with pride by the confident pre-
diction that without doubt Tom would "make a
famous man, and a reputation to his country." After
the battle of Bergen, Lord Sandwich called Lieutenant
Browne to him, and gave him the highest commenda-
tion. He said that he was "the only man who stuck

closely and boldly" to his captain to the last, after
so many of his men were killed, and that "he could
not have well known what to do without him."
Tom had also become a close reader at sea, making a
study of Homer and Juvenal, and of Lucan, who was
particularly to his taste.   The proud and happy father
was certain that his beloved Tom was "like to proceed
not only a noble navigator, but a great scholar, which
will be much to your honour and my satisfaction and
content."   But now, at the threshold of so glittering a
career, a curtain falls, and we never hear again of this
gallant and admirable young man.   The last news is
that, in the summer of 1667, Sir Thomas Allen dis-
suades him from leaving the sea, which his gifts and
opportunities are tempting him to do.   The admiral
tries "by encouragement and preferment" to hold him
to the fleet.   We only know that he died, but when
or where or how is matter of pure conjecture, and was
probably unknown even to his heart-broken father and
mother.   That he was

> " Summoned to the deep,
> He, he and all his mates, to keep
> An incommunicable sleep "

is in the highest degree probable.

During Tom's three years' absence at sea, not much
of importance seems to have happened to the household
at Norwich.   In December 1664, Browne was admitted
an honorary fellow of the College of Physicians, re-
ceiving six months later his diploma.   He was now in
relation with the Royal Society, of which however,
as has been said, he never became a fellow.   Robert
Boyle, in particular, applauded his "integrity in re-
porting, as well as capacity in making experiments,"

but Browne was not invited to join the body of philosophers. In September 1665 the plague came to
Norwich, and Browne hurried the ladies of his household off to Claxton, he himself intending, if the
epidemic grew really serious, "to remove three or
four miles off," and visit his country patients from
that point. I cannot help conjecturing that he took
this opportunity to make the only foreign excursion
of which we hear in his mature days. Of this we
should know nothing if Johann Gründahl had not
stated that he met Browne at the house of a friend, at
Vorburg,[1] and that he was thus led to read and translate his works. Gründahl's Dutch edition of the works
belongs to the year 1668, but his version of the *Religio
Medici* is somewhat earlier. There is evidence of a
recrudescence in public curiosity about Browne in
Germany, France, and Holland in 1665, and several
persons are more or less vaguely described as translating, or talking about translating, his works, at that
time. Perhaps all this was stimulated by his visit to
the Continent, of which, however, all details seem to be
lost. The plague, meanwhile, which had been brought
from Yarmouth, raged at Norwich, and over three thousand citizens died within a year. It did not completely
cease until 1667. It was followed, in 1669, by a terrible
epidemic of smallpox, which attacked three hundred
Norwich households in one fortnight. These events
must have kept the old physician amply occupied, and
may partly account for his apparent neglect of literature.

---

[1] But what is "Vorburg"? Is Warburg intended? A *vorburg*
is simply a suburb. Does Gründahl mean that he met Browne at
Voorburg, the village just outside The Hague, on the Leyden road,
where (by the way) Spinoza was at that time residing?

The elder of Browne's sons had now entirely devoted
himself to science. He had developed early into a
man of considerable scholarship and unusual mental
energy. According to Wilkin, he was incorporated
of Merton College, Oxford, in June 1666, and took
his degree of doctor of physic on the 4th of July
1667, being immediately afterwards elected a fellow
of the Royal Society. It is probable that he resided
at Norwich, helping his father in his practice, until
August 1668, when the passion for travel, which was
innate in Edward Browne, seized him with violence.
He went over from Yarmouth to Rotterdam, apparently intending to go to Amsterdam, and shortly
return, but once abroad, the genius of wandering took
possession of him. He wrote very copious and punctual letters to his father, a large number of which
have been printed, while others exist in manuscript.
At Amsterdam he heard that a translation of the
Vulgar Errors into Low Dutch was completed, and
already being printed. He went on to Brussels, and
is next heard from at Vienna, proposing to go to
Venice by way of Hungary. His father was distressed
at his making excursions "so remote and chargeable,"
but sends long letters full of local news, most of which,
marvellously, seem to have reached their destination.
"Myself and all your friends do heartily wish you
would not so much as think" of prolonging the journey
to Poland, Hungary, or Turkey. "For many reasons,
we all wish you in England" (December 15, 1668),
which may be an allusion to the disappearance or death
of Tom. "Believe it, no excursion into Pol., Hung., or
Turkey adds advantage or reputation to a scholar."

But Edward had the bit between his teeth, and no

entreaties could induce him to return. A suggestion
that he should inquire into the mineral wealth of
Hungary decided him.   In April he got back to Vienna
after a harsh and laborious but very successful journey
through the Hungarian and Carinthian mining provinces. By June he was in Venice, and was being urged
by Lord Leslie to undertake a tour in Turkey. This
he refuses to do, but his anxious father (June 25)
entreats him to "maintain a *tranquillitas* and smooth-
ness of mind, which will better conserve to health."
Certainly Edward, though not tranquil, did everything
he could to amuse and please his parents, sending
home, among other presents, a *hortus siccus* of six
hundred species of plants from the garden at Padua.
All this journeying, however, was a very great expense
to his father, of which Edward is dutifully cognisant,
and full of "thanks for your long-continued indulgence."   On the way back, however, in spite of all, he
made a bolt for the irresistible East, and passed
through Bohemia and Thessaly into Turkey. At this
Thomas Browne was much displeased, and alarmed,
and when the incorrigible traveller returned to
Vienna in October, he found letters from his father
commenting severely on his "rashness and obstinate
folly."   Edward's coaxing reply is very amusing: —

"I have divers things to write to you, sir, concerning
Turkia; but I will not trouble you, sir, too much at once.
I know, sir, that you cannot but reasonably be offended with
my long stay abroad, especially in countries of small literature, but I hope that your displeasure will not continue, and
that you will add this to the rest of your great goodness and
indulgence to me, to pardon my rashness, and the expense I
have put you to. My duty to my most dear mother, and
love to my sisters and friends."

Thomas Browne, finding that Edward had observed so many novel and curious objects, had written to him to suggest that he should contribute to the *Proceedings* of the Royal Society. Edward lost no time in writing from Vienna, on the 6th of December 1668, to the secretary of the Society, Dr. Oldenburg, with whom it appears he had as yet no personal acquaintance. He told him of his opportunities, and offered his services. This letter was read before the Society on the 31st of December, and approved of. Oldenburg, although overwhelmed with correspondence, warmly encouraged Browne to communicate his mineralogical observations, and in January he forwarded, as was the wont of the Royal Society in such cases, a long string of scientific queries. During the year 1669 Edward was in constant correspondence with Oldenburg. There exist in the archives of the Royal Society a large number of letters from Edward Browne, and among them I have been so fortunate as to discover four notes from Sir Thomas Browne himself. These are dated May 31, July 10 and 28, and October 25, 1669. They are of the nature of covering letters and contain nothing of particular personal interest. The first describes Edward's tour in Hungary, and in all the writer is most anxious to emphasise his son's activity and merit. They are all docketed by Oldenburg, — to whom they were addressed, "at his house in the Palmal in St. James's Field," — as written by Dr. T. Browne, "concerning his son's mineral collections in his travels."

In the third of these letters, Thomas Browne says, "I shall, God willing, continue to serve [the Royal Society] in any way of my mean power." This is a strong hint, but Oldenburg does not respond to it.

There is a somewhat curious change of tone in the notes. In May, Oldenburg is his " worthy friend," but we gain the impression that the secretary thought Browne too eager, and snubbed him. In each letter the old physician's tone becomes less easy and familiar, and in October he is extremely deprecatory, and, with almost too much respect, he signs himself Oldenburg's " very humble servant." The discovery of these documents, of slight value in themselves, adds to our impression that Browne was exceedingly anxious to be elected to the Royal Society, as his son Edward Browne, and his disciple Henry Power, had been, but that the Council was determined that he should not have their diploma, and resolutely disregarded his hints and his civilities.[1]

In spite of all his protestations, Edward Browne made no effort to hasten home from Vienna; and it was not until Christmas 1669, after an absence of nearly eighteen months, that he presented himself at last, in a vessel from Cuxhaven, on the shores of Norfolk. He published an interesting account of his travels in 1673, and another in 1677, as well as a *History of the Cossacks* in 1672. His various writings were collected in 1685. His communications to the Philosophical Transactions of the Royal Society were frequent from 1669 onwards; and Thomas Browne had every reason to be proud of his energetic and accomplished son, who now settled down to help him

[1] My best thanks are due to Sir Archibald Geikie for his kindness in allowing me to examine and transcribe these documents, which have not been printed, nor, so far as I know, described, even by Wilkin. The very old-fashioned handwriting of Thomas Browne offers a curious contrast to the trim, modern, and legible style of his son Edward.

in his medical practice at Norwich, relieved by frequent excursions to London and to the Continent.
Later on, from 1675, Edward took a London practice
and a house in Salisbury Court, becoming, partly, it
is said, through his intimacy with one of the king's
mistresses, physician to Charles ii. He had, however,
married in 1672 Henrietta Terne, daughter of the
celebrated medical lecturer, Christopher Terne (1620–
1673), and seems to have enjoyed a domestic happiness
like that of his own father. Long before his own
death, Thomas Browne had the pleasure of seeing his
beloved son take his place as one of the most prosperous and distinguished physicians of his time. To
us, Edward Browne has become shadowy and unin-
teresting, but it is probable that to the majority of
fashionable people in London, Sir Thomas Browne
was chiefly known, at the time of his death, as the
father of the celebrated traveller and man of science,
Dr. Edward Browne of Salisbury Court.

While Edward Browne was abroad, he directed
some of his letters to the care of his sister Anne, who
was then living, or staying, with some relatives of
the name of Barker, in Clerkenwell. The Hon. Henry
Fairfax, second son of Thomas, Viscount Fairfax of
Emly, had married Frances Barker; she is the "Madam
Fairfax," of Edward's correspondence. Henry Fairfax,
who had died in 1656, had left a son, Henry, and
in 1669 he married Sir Thomas Browne's daughter
Anne. Madam Fairfax died in the same year, and we
may conjecture that it was the breaking up of the
home in Clerkenwell which led Henry and Anne
Fairfax to pay a lengthy visit to her parents in
Norwich, where their first child, Barker Fairfax, was

born, and died in the course of 1670. From Anne
Browne are lineally descended the present heads of
two noble families, the Earls of Buchan and the
Barons Erskine. Some part of her life was spent by
Anne Browne in France, in company with one of her
sisters.

A considerable stir was caused in Norfolk by a tour
through the county taken by the king and queen in
the autumn of 1671. On the 28th of September,
accompanied by the Dukes of York, Monmouth, and
Buckingham, the royal party entered Norwich. At
Trowse Bridge they were met by the mayor, with the
regalia, all the sheriffs and the aldermen, new-clothed
in scarlet, and the leading citizens, of whom Dr.
Browne was one. The civic procession turned and
conducted their Majesties to the Duke's Palace, where
they were magnificently entertained by Henry, Lord
Howard of Castle Rising, a man who represented all
that was most enlightened and intellectual in the
society of Norfolk. He was the brother of the reign-
ing duke, but a man of infinitely greater energy and
resource; he succeeded him as sixth duke in 1677.
He held a kind of state in Norwich every year, and
accounts of his liberal and splendid entertainments
occur in Edward Browne's journals. On the 29th of
September the king proceeded to the Cathedral, where
he was received by the bishop, and was sung into
church with an anthem. After service, he rode from
the Guild Hall to the New Hall, and was there feasted
by the city. After the banquet, the king expressed
his wish to knight a prominent citizen, as a memento
of his visit to Norwich. He was proceeding to confer
this honour on Thomas Thacker, the mayor, when that

worthy modestly and humbly begged that it might be
given to the most eminent inhabitant of the city, indicating the author of *Religio Medici*. The king was
graciously pleased to consent, and the physician, kneel-
ing, rose Sir Thomas Browne.[1]

This royal visit to Norfolk had the consequence of
bringing Browne into personal contact with an old and
valued correspondent. The king went back to Newmarket, and during the royal visit, the Lord Chamber-
lain, the Earl of Arlington, invited John Evelyn to join
the revels. While he was there, Lord Howard came
over to Newmarket, and must needs have Evelyn go
back with him to Norwich; he added, as an inducement,
that he should see " that famous scholar and physician,"
the author of the *Vulgar Errors*. This was more than
Evelyn could resist, and accordingly, on the 17th of
October, " thither went my Lord and I, alone, in his
flying chariot with six horses." Arriving at the Ducal
Palace in Norwich, Lord Howard " made very much "
of his distinguished guest, and, indeed, fairly tired him
out with all that he made him do in the way of sight-
seeing. On the morning of the 18th, Evelyn was
taken by Lord Howard to wait upon Sir Thomas
Browne, and his entry in his *Diary* is a precious
vignette of the surroundings of our physician's life in
Norwich: —

[1] From a letter of Sir Thomas Browne to his son Edward it
would appear, though there is some ambiguity in the language,
that the king came to Browne's house, and witnessed the dis-
section of a dolphin. There would be nothing extraordinary
in this, for Charles II.'s curiosity about all scientific experiments was notorious, and we can have no question that
Browne's reputation had reached him before he came to
Norwich.

" His whole house and garden being a paradise and cabinet
of rarities, and that of the best collection, especially medals,
books, plants, and natural things.   Amongst other curiosities,
Sir Thomas had a collection of the eggs of all the fowl and
birds he could procure, that country (especially the promon-
tory of Norfolk) being frequented, as he said, by several
kinds which seldom or never go farther into the land, as
cranes, storks, eagles, and variety of water-fowl.   He led me
to see all the remarkable places of this ancient city, being one
of the largest, and certainly, after London, one of the noblest
of England, for its venerable cathedral, number of stately
churches, cleanness of the streets, and buildings of flint so
exquisitely headed and squared, as I was much astonished at ;
but he told me they had lost the art of squaring the flints, in
which they so much excelled, and of which the churches, best
houses and walls are built.   The Castle is an antique extent
of ground, which now they call Marsfield, and would have
been a fitting area to have placed the Ducal Palace in.   The
suburbs are large, the prospects sweet, with other amenities,
not omitting the flower-gardens, in which all the inhabitants
excel."

Next day, Evelyn travelled to Euston, and so back
to Newmarket. It does not appear that he ever saw
Browne again.

From this time until his death, the life of Sir
Thomas Browne became more sequestered than ever.
He was now wealthy, his daughters were well married,
his son highly prosperous; it is evident that he with-
drew from the active part of his profession, and
devoted himself more and more entirely to literature
and science. It seems that he grew somewhat pietistic ;
and it is to these years that we must attribute the
composition of *A Letter to a Friend* and *Christian Morals*,
in whose gravity we seem to have proceeded far from
the sprightly adolescence of *Religio Medici*. In 1676
we find Browne warning his son Edward against

yielding to the fascination of Lucretius. Of the *De
Rerum Natura*, which delighted such contemporaries as
Evelyn, and even Jeremy Taylor, Sir Thomas Browne
can now only say, "I do not much recommend the
reading or studying of it, there being divers impieties
in it, and 'tis no credit to be punctually versed in it."
Thomas Tenison, a prodigy of the Norwich grammar
school, who was much in Sir Thomas Browne's household, and who had already cheerily confuted Hobbes,
has written "a good poem" against the Lucretians of
this age, in imitation of the *De Rerum Natura*, "in a
manuscript dedicated to me." This was the Tenison
who was afterwards editor of Browne's posthumous
tracts, and from 1694 onwards Archbishop of Canter-
bury.

About 1675, a new inmate of the house at Norwich
was Edward Browne's little son, Thomas, now three
years old. The London air did not suit him at
Salisbury Court, and the grandparents were only too
glad of the child's company. From this time forward
the references to "little Tomey" are constant. He
"is lively, God be thanked. He lieth with Betty.
She takes great care of him, and gets him to bed
in due time, for he riseth early. She or Frank is
fain sometimes to play him asleep with a fiddle.
When we send away our letters he scribbles a paper
and will have it sent to his sister, and sayeth she doth
not know how many fine things there are in Norwich."
They have the usual fright of grandparents, whenever
Tomey has a cold, and in one illness Sir Thomas
Browne's spelling, usually so correct, goes all to pieces
with anxiety, and tells us that the child is "much
batter of his coffe." In 1678, Tomey begins to go to

school, "and is a very good boy, and delights his
grandfather when he comes home." He grew up a
worthy scion of the stock he came from, became a
physician early, and would doubtless have been distinguished, but for an accident. In 1710, two years
after his father's death, he was thrown from his horse
and died of the injuries.

Sir Thomas Browne's health began to fail some
years before his death. In January 1679 he had a
severe illness, which had scarcely passed away, before
a fit of influenza laid the household low, sparing,
however, little Tomey. Sir Thomas's long letters to
his son Edward are full of local news and scientific
gossip, but say very little about his own doings. We
learn, however, that both grandparents are much
exercised about getting Tomey breeched against the
assizes, he being now "a beaux tall boy, and will be
much a man." In this great matter, Tomey himself
is superlatively interested, and "would give all his
stock to see his breeches," over which the tailor
culpably dawdles. So life went gently and merrily
on in the Norwich household, until Tomey was ten
years old, the grandfather growing, we suppose, ever
a little quieter and weaker, but retaining all cheerfulness and his intellectual vivacity. He had made
his will in December 1679, but it was not until
October 19, 1682, that a sharp attack of colic carried
him off, after a short illness. He had enjoyed the
great pleasure of living to see his beloved son
Edward made physician to St. Bartholomew's Hospital,
at the express desire of the king. This appointment
was dated the 7th of September, and news of it must
have reached Norwich about a month before Browne's

death. It is a curious reflection that Sir Thomas
Browne, who seems to us the happiest and the most
prosperous of men, suffered from an occasional
melancholy in which he longed to die. He could even
say, "I think no man ever desired life, as I have sometimes death." He had written, in *Religio Medici*, that
for the tail of the snake to return into its mouth
precisely at the day of a man's nativity, "is indeed a
remarkable coincidence." It occurred in his own case,
for he died on his seventy-seventh birthday. Lady
Browne survived her husband until February 24, 1685.

CHAPTER VI

POSTHUMOUS WRITINGS — PERSONAL CHARACTER-
ISTICS

AFTER 1658 Sir Thomas Browne published nothing
new, although he was frequently called upon to super-
intend fresh issues of his earlier works, which retained
their popularity to the full. Since 1659 these had
appeared in a single folio volume, of which an edition
was corrected by the author in 1682, just before his
death. The last imprint of *Religio Medici* seen by the
author was called the eighth, but was in reality at
least the fourteenth. The *Vulgar Errors* had been
printed five times, *Urn-Burial* and *The Garden of Cyrus*
four times, before the death of Browne. In the face
of so remarkable and so long sustained a success, it is
strange that he refrained from fresh publication during
the last quarter of a century of his life, especially as
he wrote during part of that time rather abundantly.
After his death, a large quantity of manuscripts came
into the hands of Lady Browne and her son, Edward,
who sought in vain for any instructions about them.
But Sir Thomas had never said what he wished to be
done, "either for the suppressing or the publishing of
them." The executors placed them, as they were, in
the hands of Thomas Tenison. It is possible that
Lady Browne had scruples against publication, for it

was not until a month or two before her death that
anything fresh appeared.

At length, in 1684, Tenison produced a small octavo,
entitled *Certain Miscellany Tracts,* and this was the
earliest instalment of Browne's posthumous writings.
These tracts were appended to the *Works* in 1686, and
henceforth formed a part of them.   Tenison tells us
that he selected them out of many disordered papers,
and arranged them as best he could.   We gather that
they had all been sent at one time or another, in the
form of letters, to persons such as Evelyn, Dugdale,
Lord Yarmouth, Sir Nicholas Bacon, and perhaps
Edward Browne.   They are thirteen in number, and
very diverse in subject, length, and importance.
Most of them were obviously written, in reply to the
queries of friends, in what Tenison aptly calls " those
little spaces of vacancy which [Browne] snatched from
the very many occasions which gave him hourly in-
terruption."   In several instances, we can trace by
internal evidence the occasions upon which the particular essays were written, and those addressed to
Evelyn on gardens and to Dugdale on the fen-country
have already been mentioned in the course of this
narrative.

The important treatise on "Plants mentioned in
Scripture" is almost long enough to form a little
volume.   It was dedicated to Sir Nicholas Bacon,
whose passion for flowers we have already recorded.
From the purely zoological essays we learn that that
beautiful bird the hoopoe was common in Norfolk in
Browne's day, so common that the naturalist cannot
understand its being unfamiliar to a correspondent
in another part of England.   The other essays, on

cymbals, on rhopalic (or club-shaped) verses, on the primitive language, on the fishes eaten by our Saviour after His resurrection, on artificial mounts or barrows, and on the site of Troy, are curious and trifling examples of the wit of the day, not very important to us nor highly characteristic of the genius of their author. They give fresh evidence, if we needed any, of the vast range of Browne's reading, which embraced at least six modern languages.

In more than one of these miscellanies, he testifies to his admiration for Rabelais, of whom, moreover, he had composed, in old French, an imitation, which was printed by Wilkin: this is a miracle of obscure ingenuity. Perhaps the most amusing of all these tracts is the last, " Museum Clausum," which is intended, as Warburton was the first in observing, to rival Rabelais's catalogue of imaginary volumes in the library of St. Victor.[1] Browne draws up a highly entertaining list of books, antiquities, pictures, and rarities of several kinds, " scarce or never " seen by mortal eye. Among them is a treatise on dreams by King Mithridates ; a collection of the writings in Hebrew, Greek, and Latin of an imaginary little girl of eight years old (this, no doubt, was a joke at the expense of Maria Schuurman) ; the works of Confucius, translated into Spanish ; a painting of Thyestes, taken at the moment when he was told at table that he had just eaten a piece of his own son ; a battle between frogs and mice, carved upon

---

[1] It appears to me likely that Tract VIII., " Of Languages " was written in, or soon after, 1653, when the publications of Sir Thomas Urquhart drew attention, not merely to the peculiarities of the style of Rabelais, but also to a scheme for a universal language. Browne had probably just read the *Logopandecteision* when he wrote his essay.

the jaw-bone of a pike; and a transcendent perfume made of all the richest odorates of both the Indies, and kept in a box made of the Muschine stone of Marienburg. All these, and other still more remarkable curiosities, are easily to be found, no doubt, by those who can tell what songs the sirens sang. "He who knows where all this treasure now is," says Sir Thomas Browne, "is a great Apollo. I'm sure I am not he."

Tenison had stated that other discourses by Browne remained in manuscript, but added that he proposed to publish them at due intervals, so that each publication might "follow rather than stifle" the tracts already issued. Accordingly, it was not until 1690 that he produced in folio a little work of great importance, *A Letter to a Friend*, a treatise which some of Browne's most judicious admirers have not hesitated to place on the highest level of his compositions. Pater has gone so far as to describe it as "perhaps, after all, the best justification of Browne's literary reputation, as it were his own curiously-figured urn, and treasure-place of immortal memory." Pater believed this "elfin *Letter*," as he calls it, to have been written as a prelude to *Urn-Burial*, and therefore in 1658; when the Oxford critic wrote, Greenhill had not yet developed that ingenious chain of evidence which makes it almost certain that *A Letter to a Friend* was composed in 1672. The stylistic fact remains the same, however, and was correctly noted by Pater, — the *Letter*, though written at a much later date, recurs to the noble temper and to the singular elation of spirit which made *Urn-Burial* and parts even of *The Garden of Cyrus* unique in English prose.

Each of the principal works of Browne has a strange uniqueness, a character which distinguishes it not merely from the writings of others, but from other writings by the same hand. Baldly stated, the subject of *A Letter to a Friend* is a page from the note-book of a country practitioner. He whose whole life is spent in witnessing the fluctuations of disease, and its termination in death, will, on one occasion only, pause to record, step by step, and with perfect sincerity of touch, the progress and character of that scene of mortal decay. His diagnosis takes the form of a letter to a person at a distance, describing to him the case of a patient who was known to them both, but whom the recipient of the letter had not lately seen. In the solemn arrangement of the address, the reader may suspect that something is fictitious, but it is not so; this is merely the result of Browne's sententious mode of approach. It is quite obvious that the "case" is a genuine one; that some real man of importance in the county had died of the maladies and under the conditions which the physician minutely describes. He was not, we gather, one of Browne's old familiar patients, since the doctor was called in when it was already too late to try to save the patient's life, when all that medicine could do was to prolong the struggle and to alleviate the distress. When he visited him first, the doctor perceived that death was in the face, and he frankly told the family so. The sick man would not see another summer, he declared, and in fact he lived not until the middle of May.

But during these last months, or weeks, Sir Thomas Browne watched his patient closely, and he made a variety of acute observations which were metaphysical

as well as physical. The first of these was that those
who love a dying person are abandoned, in his decline,
by all those intuitions which, in health, they fancy
will come to warn them of a danger. The patient
was surrounded by watchers, yet not one of them was
instructed " by dreams, thoughtful whisperings, mer-
curisms, aery nuncios or sympathetical insinuations "
of the enormous change which was imminent. The
physical crisis is attended by physical signs, and before
the approach of disease the fallacies of the imagination
withdraw: It is not from visions of the night, but
from the wasted hand, the pallid face, the haggard eye,
and from the experience of the physician interpreting
these, that we look for information. The dying man
had suffered in his childhood from rickets, and this
had left a constitutional weakness; merely to look
at him, as he lay in bed, was to expect " a withered
pericardium in this exuccous corpse." Browne spares
us none of the symptoms of the illness ; he dwells upon
them deliberately and with a professional insistency;
because he is about to lift us into a height of spiritual
ecstasy, and he wishes that leap to be taken from a
firm corporeal basis, not from a groundwork of superstition or sentiment. By gradations of disease, earnestly considered, he leads us to the article of death,
which is thus described : —

"Though we could not have his life, yet we missed not our
desires in his soft departure, which was scarce an exhalation ;
and his end not unlike his beginning, when the salient point
scarce affords a sensible motion; and his departure so like
unto sleep, that he scarce needed the civil ceremony of closing
his eyes; contrary unto the common way, wherein Death
draws up, Sleep lets fall the eyelids. With what strife and
pains we came into the world we know not, but 'tis commonly

no easy matter to get out of it. Yet, if it could be made out that those who have easy nativities have commonly hard deaths, and contrarily, his departure was so easy, that we might justly suspect his birth was of another nature, and that some Juno sat cross-legged at his nativity."

In this, and in all that led up to it, there is observable a deep stoic tone, which little resembles the slightly hysteric manner in which death is described by most of Browne's contemporaries. There is plenty of sympathy, and of sorrow, in the terms of the *Letter to a Friend*, but there is no waste of sentiment. We feel that for a Christian philosopher, who is also a broad-minded physicist, to neglect the idea of death, would be contemptible. Yet, as Browne had himself said long before, a constant familiarity with its phenomena, and the conjunction of professional ideas with them, tends to smooth away the salient parts of thought, so that it is not to an elderly doctor that we should be apt to go for fresh impressions about the progress of dissolution down to death, because his attention has been worn away, and the subject has become commonplace to him. Well, Sir Thomas Browne, an old country practitioner, now approaching his seventieth year, will, once for all, set down his impressions, to see whether they really are so dulled and smooth as he fears may be the case. He will see whether he cannot still hold a middle course between the foolish terror of the inexperienced, and that *nonchalance bestiale* which Montaigne notes in those whom constant practice has made indifferent to the images of death.

He is rewarded by a poignant originality, by a singular freshness of aptitude. There is none of the careless and vague conventionality which he feared to

meet with. In this case of the dying friend, which
presents nothing of supreme scientific curiosity, all
Browne's life-long experience seems concentrated, so
that we have his reflections not on this alone, but on
all that life has taught him about disease, all that it
has made him hope for in the beautiful advances
of " soft death."   In the extenuation of this particular
patient, the spiritual part of his appearance became
greatly emphasised.   His countenance grew more
and more refined and distinguished as he grew
thinner and weaker; at last, Browne exclaims, " I
never more lively beheld the starved characters of
Dante in any living face."   He goes backward to
discuss what inward changes answered to this outward
refinement; but again he has to warn us against vain
and superstitious fancies, commoner then than they
are now : —

" I could not but take notice how his female friends were
irrationally curious so strictly to examine his dreams, and in
this low state to hope for the phantasms of health.   He was
now past the healthful dreams of the sun, moon, and stars, in
their clarity and proper causes.   'T was too late to dream of
flying, of limpid fountains, smooth waters, white vestments,
and fruitful green trees, which are the visions of healthful
sleeps, and at good distance from the grave."

Having firmly placed the phenomena with which he
has been dealing on a physical footing, and having
rejected, with an uncommon resolution, all the temptations which astrology throws out " to entitle the
stars unto any concern of his death," Browne calls
upon us to slip, as it were unconsciously, from the contemplation of this gracious and appropriate method of
decease, to that of the eternal mystery of life of which

it was the antechamber. His idea is that the spirit
died, that is to say became immortal, sooner than the
body ceased to breathe, and that therefore the transi-
tion on the threshold of eternity was gradual, and the
transformation to be piously and carefully observed.
At this point, the character of *A Letter to a Friend*
loses its peculiar value, and becomes merged, in a
curious way, for which the inedited state of the
manuscript is certainly responsible, in the last work of
Browne which we are called upon to analyse, the
Christian Morals.

After the death of Browne's only son in 1708, and
the final extinction of the male line by that of his
grandson in 1710, his manuscript papers seem to have
come into the possession of his daughter Elizabeth,
who had married, about 1680, Captain George Lyttelton
of Guernsey. The first step which she took, acting
under the advice of Archbishop Tenison, was to issue
a collection of *Posthumous Works.* Among these, two
are of particular, though hardly of absorbing, interest.
The essay on *Brampton Urns*, written in 1668, is a
supplement to the *Urn-Burial* of 1658, and should be
printed with it. It describes an important discovery
of ancient vessels, made in a large field between Buxton
Lammas and Brampton, on the Bure, to the north of
Norwich. Browne " thought he had taken leave of
urns," but could not forbear to expatiate on these,
at the digging out of which he himself was present.
The account of these antiquities is written with a
simplicity and a straightforwardness very unusual in
Browne, who has adorned it with none of his magnificent verbiage and none of his splendid reflections.
It is probably, in spite of a certain fulness, no more

than a set of notes taken down to aid his memory. We see him, in the mind's eye, standing in the wet ploughed field at Brampton, watching the excavation with eager eyes, and driven nearly to frenzy by the clumsiness of the labourers. The ground was soft with rain, and when the men used their picks, the urns were revealed, but, at first, "earnestly and carelessly digging, they broke all they met with, and finding nothing but ashes and burnt bones, they scattered what they found." Nor even when Browne hung over them, directing their labours, were matters much better, for "though I met with two [urns] in the side of the ditch, and used all care I could with the workmen, yet they were broken." Here again we meet with that strange fantasy, that the wine buried long ages ago must retain its gust and virtue immensely heightened. Nothing annoyed Browne more at Brampton than that the labourers should have broken divers glasses that probably contained liquors.

The tract named *Repertorium* was a disappointment to Browne's admirers. It appears to have been known in the physician's lifetime that he was preparing an exhaustive account of the monuments in the Cathedral Church of Norwich. He is believed to have put his desultory notes together in the form of the *Repertorium* as late as 1682, during the last months of his life, for it records the death of his old friend, Hezekiah Burton, prebendary of Norwich since 1667, who died in 1681. Those who imagined that the *Repertorium* would be, what Browne might easily have made it, a grandiose and melodious reverie among the tombs of an ancient minster, were greatly displeased to find such a prosaic inventory of monuments as any careful antiquary could draw up.   Nor is it, we are told, so minute or so trustworthy as to be very useful for the prosaic purpose for which it was intended.   John Bagford, the bibliographical shoemaker, frowned upon it at its birth by saying that it "rather feared than deserved publication," and it remains an instance of the necessity that Browne's work had of being duly robed, jewelled, and perfumed before it was presented to the public.

The famous physician had now, when the *Posthumous Works* were issued in 1712, been dead for thirty years, and there was still a legend that his writings were not complete.   There were those yet living who remembered that he had engaged his last years in the preparation of an ethical work which he designed to complete what was imperfect in *Religio Medici*. Elizabeth Lyttelton, in particular, had a clear recollection of reading the manuscript of such a work, before she left home in 1680, and when it was fresh from her father's pen.   Dr. John Jeffery, archdeacon of Norwich, had read it soon after Browne's death ; and he and the family had the conviction that it had been placed, together with the rest of Browne's voluminous manuscripts, in the hands of Archbishop Tenison.   He, however, could not recover a trace of it, and it was given up for lost until the death of the archbishop in December 1715.   His successor in the primacy, William Wake, when search among Tenison's papers was being made in his presence, detected what could only be the lost manuscript of Sir Thomas Browne.   He immediately sent it, with a letter, to Mrs. Lyttelton, who passed it on to Archdeacon Jeffery to be edited.   John Jeffery was now one of the last survivors among those

who had known Browne intimately. A Suffolk man
by birth, the reputation of his eloquence and piety
had led to his being invited to Norwich in 1678, when
the parishioners of St. Peter Mancroft, of whom Sir
Thomas Browne was the most distinguished, elected
him to that living.

The treasure trove was published at Cambridge in
1716, under the title of *Christian Morals*, with prefaces
signed by Elizabeth Lyttelton and by John Jeffery.
The publication was dedicated by Mrs. Lyttelton, in
affectionate terms, to David Erskine, Earl of Buchan,
who had married in 1697 the daughter of Henry
Fairfax of Hurst, and who was therefore closely connected with the family of Sir Thomas Browne. Lord
Buchan, who was only ten years old when the physician
died, would not be one of those who recollected him at
Norwich. The book was divided — presumably by the
author, since Jeffery disowns any manipulation — into
three parts. The first of these is nothing more nor
less than the closing pages of *A Letter to a Friend*,
much expanded and adorned. The second is concerned
with the criticism of opinion ; the third collects a series
of principles for the conduct of life. The *Christian
Morals* is a work innocent of all evolution ; it begins
anywhere and closes nowhere.   It is a string of
pleasant gnomic expansions, and excellent hortatory
remarks. Common sense is set out in it with all the
trappings of an extremely elaborate style. The author
speaks like a sibylline oracle, addressing us from a
great height of experience. The hard light of his
precepts, and it is very dry, is softened by an
extreme, sometimes an excessive, elegance of expression.   The book is an address, in the manner of

N

Solomon, to anybody, and that autobiographical air of confidence, which was so fascinating in *Religio Medici*, is here wholly relinquished in favour of doctrine and admonishment. The writer whom we have loved to find walking by our side, and "murmuring like a noon-tide bee," has ascended the pulpit in a cassock, and thunders his *Christian Morals* at us from a height above our heads.

No one has loved Browne better than Greenhill did, and since he says that this book "by its title raises expectations which are hardly realised," and that it "contains nothing equal in piety or eloquence" to the author's best things elsewhere, we are absolved from any extravagance of admiration for *Christian Morals*. It belongs to a class of hortatory treatises which were popular in the seventeenth century, and are out of fashion now, while in that very class it had predecessors of a greater consistency and a livelier eloquence. For instance, one would put it down at any moment to take up George Montagu's *Manchester al Mondo*, with which it courts, but cannot sustain, comparison. This kind of book, occupied with the sententious expansion of accepted moral maxims, is scarcely compatible with high intellectual culture. It is in its essence primitive, and pleases now, if it please at all, by its quaintness and naïveté. It belonged to a social order which had thought for a century that all wisdom, human and divine, was shut up within the *Quatrains* of the Lord of Pibrac, which were household words in every European language. There is good reason to suppose that in Browne's case the treatise consists of paragraphs extended from thoughts set down at intervals in a common-place book.

It is evident that *Christian Morals* is a work of the close of its author's life. What is said, and frequently repeated, about the latitude of years and the deep gust of the world, points to an age of seventy years and over. It is not likely that, in its present form, it was begun before 1675, nor finished earlier than 1680. It has something of the triteness of old age, and, at the same time, much of its serenity and dignity. It is a call from a venerable man to " behold thyself by inward optics, and the crystalline of thy soul." It breathes a full sense of the restfulness and sweetness of memory directed backwards over a long and well-spent life. It is packed with precepts which appeal to the highest sentiments of a man, and are appropriate in the mouth of one who has made them the guiding light of his own life. Among such gnomes none is better worth cherishing than the following, with which Part i. closes : —

" Bright thoughts, clear deeds, constancy, fidelity, bounty, and generous honesty are the gems of noble minds ; wherein — to derogate from none — the true heroic English gentleman hath no peer."

Perhaps the most valuable pages of *Christian Morals* are those which inculcate and define a wholesome critical attitude towards life and literature. Browne bids us avoid dogmatism, and be guided by well-weighed considerations. Here is the gnomic wisdom of the old physician at its ripest: —

" Let thy studies be free as thy thoughts and contemplations, but fly not only upon the wings of imagination. Join sense unto reason and experiment unto speculation, and so give life unto embryon truths, and verities yet in their chaos. There is nothing more acceptable unto the ingenious world than this noble eluctation of truth, wherein, against the tenacity of prejudice and prescription, this century now prevaileth.   What libraries of new volumes aftertimes will behold, and in what a new world of knowledge the eyes of our posterity may be happy, a few ages may joyfully declare, and is but a cold thought unto those who cannot hope to behold this exantlation of truth, or that obscured virgin half out of the pit."

The love of using extraordinary words to heighten the effect of ordinary thoughts was no less powerful in him at the close of his life than it had been at its beginning.   It is impossible not to ask ourselves how many of his readers Browne expected to know that "exantlation" is the same as "pumping up out of a well," and that "eluctation" means "pushing forth." Did he in the pride of his own learning forget the existence of the comparative ignorance around him, or did he consciously yield to the pleasure of dazzling the unlearned?   With one more extract we must leave *Christian Morals* to produce its own fragmentary impression : —

"Look not for whales in the Euxine Sea, or expect great matters where they are not to be found.   Seek not for profundity in shallowness, or fertility in a wilderness.   Place not the expectation of great happiness here below or think to find heaven on earth, wherein we must be content with embryon felicities and fruitions of doubtful forces.   For the circle of our felicities makes but short arches.   In every clime we are in a periscian state [that is : with shadows all about us], and with our light our shadow and darkness walk about us.   Our contentments stand upon the tops of pyramids ready to fall off, and the insecurity of their enjoyments abrupteth our tranquillities.   What we magnify is magnificent, but like to the Colossus, noble without, stuffed with rubbish and coarse metal within.   Even the sun, whose glorious outside we behold, may have dark and smoky entrails."

In all these long-drawn reflections we find little or
nothing asserted about faith or dogma. There is less,
in fact, of definite assurance in *Christian Morals* than
there had been in *Religio Medici*. But to any one who
made this objection, Browne would doubtless have
replied, as Dr. Johnson did to the Duc de Chaulnes
on a similar occasion, that all such exhortation was
taken for granted, as it is the Christian religion alone
which puts morality upon its proper basis.

Two years after the death of Sir Thomas Browne, it
was announced that a project was on foot for writing
his life. There can be no doubt that the memorials
collected by John Whitefoot were jotted down at this
time for the purpose of aiding the biographer. We
may bear with philosophy the disappointment of not
possessing this life, which was evidently never written,
since it was to have been produced at that very darkest
hour of English biography, when Sprat's *Life of Cowley*
was the model in fashion, and since unquestionably
Thomas Tenison was to have been the writer. That
archbishop was an excellent religious creature, but
when he took a pen in hand he grew, as Swift said
of him, "hot and heavy, like a tailor's goose." In all
probability, Tenison, as his duties crowded upon him,
gradually abandoned the design of writing the Life of
Browne, yet clung to it long enough to prevent its
preparation by any other writer. Soon after 1682,
however, the Rev. John Whitefoot, rector of Heigham,
in Norfolk, who had been more closely acquainted with
Browne, ever since he came to Norwich in 1637, than
any other surviving friend, put down those recollec-
tions, of which mention has just been made. We can
only wish that his modesty had permitted him to
carry them into further detail.

From this source, however, and from his portraits, we gain a distinct idea of the personal appearance of Sir Thomas Browne. He was of moderate height, and neither fat nor lean; he was εὐσάρκος, of a well-proportioned figure. He appears, from his pictures, to have had an abundance of warm-coloured hair, naturally rolling; when his tomb was opened, it was seen to be still of an auburn tint, in spite of his seventy-seven years. He wore a moustache and small chin-beard, and his complexion was "answerable to his name," being doubtless tanned by much exposure. His remarkably large and luminous eyes, dark, under curved eyebrows, gave a look of distinction and curiosity to his face; the smiling mouth, full nose and smooth forehead presented a healthful comeliness, a sense of richness in vitality, which responded to the man's amiable and wholesome disposition. He was simple in his dress, although so very fond of ornament in his style, and he "affected plainness." It was thought singular that he always wore a cloak and boots, which had been the dress of his youth, even after that style went out at the Restoration. He was subject to cold, and took pains to be always warmly clad; we have seen his solicitude that his sons should wear flannel next their skin.

In his domestic relations, Browne seems to have approached perfection. He was a constant and assiduous husband, and a most tender father, without lapsing into any foolish fondness in his discipline of his children. His letters to the various members of his family, and in particular to his sons, are full of considerate affection. More than this, they display the rare parental wisdom which recognises the

moment when the child has become adult, and must
be approached with sympathy and tact, as being a
friend and no longer a dependant. Whitefoot, who
was not a practised writer, seems to say that Browne's
chief temptations were love and anger, and that the
passions which did most easily beset him were "the
irascible and concupiscible." As, however, he also tells
us that both of these were under the control of his
reason, it is possible that Browne, as he occasionally
does even in *Religio Medici*, had confided to his friend
what a rogue he would be in grain, were it not for
the vigour of his Christian philosophy. As a fact, he
seems to have been, outwardly, the most serene and
the most amenable of citizens. "He had no despotical
power over his affections and passions, but as large a
political power over them as any stoic or man of his
time." We gain the impression that Browne sometimes boasted of his reserve, just as Wordsworth said
that he could have inflamed the passions no less tumul-
tuously than Lord Byron, if he had had a mind to
do so.

Browne's serenity was marked in his daily comport-
ment. "He was never seen to be transported with
mirth or dejected with sadness. Always cheerful, but
rarely merry." He had no sense of humour, and here
it is worth while to observe that those who are so fond
of attributing this quality to Sir Thomas Browne are
deceived by what has now come to be the quaintness
or oddity of his language. It is doubtful whether in
the whole body of his writings there is a single phrase
written for the purpose or in the expectation of raising
a laugh. He is occasionally willing to provoke a smile
by his wit, but that is a very different thing from

humour. As a man, and as a writer, he was sententious.   Whitefoot tells us that in conversation he
would rarely break into a jest, and that if he did do
so, by accident, he was wont to blush at the levity
of what he had perpetrated.   This, again, was like
Wordsworth, who had a theory that it was not becoming to allow himself to be funny.

A curious idiosyncrasy was an effect of his thin
dark skin, for blush after blush would mantle over
his face on slight occasion, and often without any
observable cause at all.   Whitefoot attributed this to
Browne's modesty, but perhaps it was merely physical; Darwin notes that this phenomenon is very frequent in mulattoes.   Browne seems to have discoursed
with great freedom and fulness when he was stirred
with excitement; but on ordinary occasions he was
"so free from loquacity, or much talkativeness, that
he was something difficult to be engaged in any
discourse; though, when he was so, it was always
singular, and never trite nor vulgar.   Parsimonious in
nothing but his time, whereof he made as much im-
provement, with as little loss, as any man in it, when
he had any to spare from his drudging practice, he
was scarce patient of any diversion from his study,
so impatient of sloth and idleness, that he would say
he 'could not do nothing.'"

Like many of those who combine high gifts of
imagination with a serene and dispassionate temperament, Browne cultivated friendship with great care.
His attitude to this virtue was very similar to that
of Montaigne.   He saw nothing in the Greek stories
of the devotion of Damon to Pythias or of Achilles to
Patroclus which he could not have performed himself.

He discovered no extravagance in the idea that a man should lay down his life for another man, if he loved him. His expressions on this subject of friendship are among the most eloquent which his writings contain, and among the most characteristic. He says : —

" With my friend I desire not to share or to participate, but to engross, his sorrows, that, by making them mine own, I may more easily discuss them. In my own reason, and within myself, I can command that which I cannot intreat without myself, and within the circle of another. I have often thought those noble pains and examples of friendship not so truly histories of what had been, as fictions of what should be ; but I now perceive nothing in them but possibilities. . . . I confess I do not observe that order that the Schools ordain our affections, to love our parents, wives, children, and then our friends. For, excepting the injunctions of religion, I do not find in myself such a necessary and indissoluble sympathy to all those of my blood. I hope I do not break the Fifth Commandment, if I conceive I may love my friend before the nearest of my blood, even those to whom I owe the principles of life. I never yet cast a true affection on a woman ; but I have loved my friend as I do virtue, my soul, my God."

This was written in 1635, and before his marriage to Dorothy Mileham. But the sentiment of friendship, moderated by age and exercised with reasonable reserve, continued dominant with him to the last.

Browne's linguistic acquirements were remarkable. In 1635 he was able to say, "besides the jargon and *patois* of several provinces, I understand no less than six languages." He must be speaking here of modern languages ; French, Italian, Spanish, German, Dutch, and Danish are probably those he refers to. He would not include Latin and Greek in such a list, nor Hebrew, of which " he was not content to be wholly ignorant," nor Arabic, which he read, although he erroneously supposed it to be "a derivative idiom" of Hebrew. His correspondence with the Icelanders was sustained in Latin, but he was perhaps not entirely ignorant of the ancient language of the island. We are told that he continued to add to his knowledge, and that he came to understand "most of the European languages, namely, all that are in Hutten's Bible, which he made use of." To pick out the meaning of a page in a polyglot Bible is no great stretch of scholarship, though it seems to have dazzled Whitefoot. It is difficult to judge how deep Browne's knowledge of languages may have been, but it was certainly wide. His letters to his sons Edward and Thomas contain some very sensible advice as to the best way of gaining colloquial freedom in a foreign tongue.

He was a constant student of astronomy, although tainted to the last by that provoking desire to obtain from the stars replies to private conundrums, which was a vice of the intelligence of the seventeenth century. "I know the names, and something more," he says, "of all the constellations in my horizon"; and no English writer has given a nobler impression of the plenitude and mystery of the nocturnal sky. How deep a study he made of zoology and of botany, his books and papers are before us to prove. Whether he had any practice in the art of music we do not know, but he used to sit in Norwich cathedral listening, in an ecstasy, to its organ, the tone of which was particularly sweet. He regretted that he did not possess one of those miraculous memories with which Scaliger was credited, which retained every fact and date that was stored up in it, but his own

was "capacious and tenacious." He never forgot the
contents of a book that he had read; was quick to
recollect all persons he had ever seen, though after a
long course of years; and instantly connected with
people's names their physical peculiarities and their
accustomed modes of address. These were character-
istics which help to explain Sir Thomas Browne's
immense popularity as a doctor.

He was excellent company when he was not distracted by his professional responsibilities. Those who
knew him only by his books were sometimes disappointed to find the man so quiet and sedate; nor did
he ever wake up in society to a high note of eloquence.
He cultivated a stoical genius, which he loved to illustrate by "excellent strains" in the poetry of Lucan.
He was plain almost to affectation; and Whitefoot has
an excellent phrase to describe his manner when he
says that it "expressed more light than heat in the
temper of his brain." He was, above all, and at all
times, a dreamer of dreams; and to complete our
picture of him we can do no better than to quote the
visionary's own charming confession:—

"At my nativity my ascendant was the watery sign of
Scorpius. I was born in the planetary hour of Saturn, and I
think I have a piece of that leaden planet in me. I am no
way facetious, nor disposed for the mirth and galliardize of
company; yet in one dream I can compose a whole comedy,
behold the action, apprehend the jests, and laugh myself
awake at the conceits thereof. Were my memory as faithful
as my reason is then fruitful, I would never study but in my
dreams; and this time also would I choose for my devotions.
But our grosser memories have then so little hold of our
abstracted understandings, that they forget the story, and can
only relate to our awakèd souls a confused and broken tale
of that that hath passed."

CHAPTER VII

LANGUAGE AND INFLUENCE

A CURIOUS element in Browne's intellectual situation
was its isolated character. Others had London to look
to, or at least Oxford or Cambridge; he had only
Norwich, and although that city possessed a large
population and much comparative dignity, there was
no rivalry for him there and little encouragement.
For these he was forced to turn to disciples and corre-
spondents; and we form the impression that, as time
went by, he got less and less stimulus from the one
and from the other. In the later years, Browne's
main intellectual solace came from the piety, the zeal,
the untiring kindliness, of his admirable son Edward,
who shared from London with his father in Norwich
all that was curious and interesting in the movement
of science. But Edward Browne, a true child of the
new age, was entirely devoted to the advancement of
exact knowledge. He wanted to add to the store of
facts, to discover the precise proportions of truth; to
lay down the principles of the New Philosophy, as his
friends had called it when they met so soberly, so
stringently, at those lodgings of Dr. Goddard's, over
the optician's shop in Wood Street, out of which the
Royal Society had sprung. Edward Browne excluded
the imagination altogether from his speculations; the

188

light he worked in was a dry, white light.   But the
light in which Thomas Browne worked was shot with
all the colours of the spectrum, it was flashed out
against a firmament of romantic gloom.   Edward's
ambition was to get at the fact, to fasten it down with
the fewest words possible, with a disregard for any
quality of style except a lucid brevity.   In a generation so given over to parsimony of effect, what comfort
was there left for the embroidering visionary who had
written the *Urn-Burial*?

But his very provincialism and absence of rivalry
brought Browne consolations.   He was a very great
man at Norwich, whatever might be thought of him
in London.   He seems to have been little troubled by
that oppression of spirits which the vastness of possible
attainment breeds in men of really encyclopædic
ambition.   He became, in the absence of criticism at
his side, satisfied with short draughts of that Pierian
spring of which Pope, another hasty drinker, speaks
so sententiously.   The age of book-learning for its
own sake was just over; the sixteenth century had
carried the pursuit of that kind of learning to the last
extremity, in an age when Salmasius had suffered the
torments of Tantalus because he was not able to read
all books at once.   The new age was disregarding
books, and was going straight to nature, determined to
make new, stiff, half-mathematical treatises that should
be mere records of experiment, repertories of hard fact.
Sir Thomas Browne, as a scholar, comes between the
two epochs.   He had not Donne's " hydroptic immoder-
ate desire of human learning," nor was he capable, like
Ray, of putting all the beauty of erudition aside and
reducing literature to a methodical synopsis of species.

He was the greatest and the most intelligent of a little group who handled facts, but delighted to take refuge from them in speculation. Science to him, as we see in his letters to Edward Browne, was still "literature," just as it was to others in whom we now detect a certain taint of quackery, as it was pre-eminently to that curious person, John Bulwer, the "chirosopher," and author in 1650 of *Anthropometamorphosis*. The Royal Society could not recognise the erudition of such persons, however talented they might be, and however eloquent, for it had been definitely created for the purpose of sweeping them away.

We have, therefore, in considering the position of Sir Thomas Browne, to face the fact that his subject-matter is not of supreme importance, that it would, even, not be important enough to preserve him — if that were all he had to give — among the foremost literary oddities of his time. If we think of him merely as a physician or surgeon, he has no claim to be remembered by the side of such men as Sydenham or Wallis or Richard Lower. No one can seriously believe that the *Vulgar Errors* gives him a right to be ranked among biologists. We do not go to the *Urn-Burial* for information about antique ceramic, nor to *The Garden of Cyrus* for rules of horticulture, nor to *Christian Morals* for an ethical system. Wherever we lean on the substance of Browne's treatises, it cracks and gives way, it is worm-eaten and hollow. If we go to his books as to compendiums of valuable information, we find them as empty as so many leaking vessels.

Browne, therefore, is a pre-eminent example of the class of writer with whom it is form, not substance, that is of the first importance. He is interesting almost exclusively to the student and lover of style. That is to say, to the student of style in its wider acceptation, not in the mere melodious arrangement of beautiful words, but in the manipulation of language with such art as to reveal a personal temperament and to illustrate a human point of view. Among English prose-writers of the highest merit there are few who have more consciously, more successfully, aimed at the translation of temperament by style than the physician of Norwich did. His case is very curious, because we find in him little sympathy with the current literature of his country, or of the modern vernaculars at all. In his superb neglect of all contemporary poetry and prose, in his scorn of the poets in particular, he exceeds Jeremy Taylor, whose contempt of modern writing went far. The great English authors from Chaucer down to Milton, from Wycliffe down to Dryden, might never have existed for all the attention they receive from Sir Thomas Browne. Almost the only reference to a living imaginative author which is to be found in the length and breadth of his works is a note written at the time that *Hudibras* was published. That piece reminds him of " divers examples " of burlesque in Athenæus; " the first inventor hereof was Hipponactes, but Hegemon, Sopater and many more pursued the same vein." The whole note is a mere pellet of sun-dried pedantry, without a single word to show that the author had comprehended or read or perhaps even seen Butler's poem.

Where, then, did he find courage to write in the service of beauty ? Recognising no dignity in the English language, no importance or vitality in English literature, how was it that he took the trouble to clothe himself in the splendours of the one and consciously to adorn the other? These are questions which it is impossible to answer. All we can affirm is that such was the odd, the paradoxical case; that Sir Thomas Browne, profoundly indifferent to English prose other than his own, devoted himself to English prose as if it had been the art of his predilection. Unquestionably, he tasted the divine pleasure of writing for its own sake; that breathes out of all his best pages. Moreover, in spite of his unaccountable attitude to contemporary literature and his scorn of its attempts, in his own person he was confident of conquering eternity with the delicious artifice of style.

We do not begin to understand Browne, or do justice to him, until we comprehend that we are dealing with a conscious and sensitive artist. We are told that Browne was simple in his manners and attire. Let us not believe that his writing is plain or easy. The examination of his numerous manuscripts is enough to show with what care he ran over the texture of his sentences, weighing them down with precious metal, fusing, elaborating, and implicating them, turning the rough yarn of statement into heavy cloth of gold. De Quincey said that we abuse the attribution "simple"; not everything fine is simple, he says, — Belshazzar's feast was not. The style of Sir Thomas Browne is another splendid thing which, however, is not simple. Browne is distinctly a difficult writer. It is not that his thought is exceedingly profound, but it is often startlingly unexpected, and dazzles us by its flash, while it is almost always clothed in language of a wanton ingenuity. Browne introduces themes, illustrations, digressions, for their own sakes, and because they give him his opportunity to fly off, obliquely, with a flash of his unaccountable intelligence, to some distant corner of the subject. He has not the smallest reluctance in pillaging antiquity, particularly the ornate Latin of the Renaissance, to adorn his work, and he likes to hear great classic names, sonorous and obscure, reverberating down the hollow places of his prose. And, if we think of him as an architect of phrases, the skill with which he is able to build up cloud-castles of mere verbal development is positively a snare to him; he cannot stop; he will pile story upon story, and a turret on the last, and a pinnacle upon the turret. The fabric always stands there, high in air, since it is raised with cunning out of strong materials, but it is sometimes too fantastic to be habitable.

Browne was greatly interested in the beauty of words, in their sound, their form, the image that they raised. But his treatment of them was very curious, and is not easily or completely to be justified. There was something abnormal in Browne's intellect, and it is shown in the rather mad way in which he tossed words about. He was "exuberant in conceit," and this richness affected his vocabulary; it made him sometimes freakish and capricious. Dr. Johnson, who was far more thoroughly restrained by tradition, had his own tendencies to extravagance of diction, and excused them by saying, "He that thinks with more extent than another will want words of larger meaning; he that thinks with more subtlety will seek for terms of more nice discrimination." Browne, with his instinct for reducing everything in heaven or earth to the substance of the subject in hand, perpetually

Q.

"wants" words, and "seeks" them ardently. He
wants them to be above all things picturesque; he
seeks them far afield and in the most unlikely places.
He was very punctilious, as we have seen, and highly
artificial. He was conscious of no controlling taste
around him, holding him in, subduing the most daring
elements in his vocabulary. In consequence, he built
up the music of his sonorous balanced periods as he
pleased, without any criticism to restrain him, and the
consequence is the irregular splendour that we see in
the *Urn-Burial* and *A Letter to a Friend.*

These were the considerations, no doubt, which led
Coleridge, one of Browne's greatest admirers, to say
that Browne, "though a writer of great genius, first
effectually injured the literary taste of the nation by
his introduction of learned words, merely because they
were learned." The only exception we can make to
this lies in the use of "first"; Coleridge, of course,
remembered that the whole tendency of the age in
which Browne lived was towards violent experiment in
the æsthetic value of words. We see it in Burton, in
Wilkins, in Milton, but Coleridge is perfectly right
in emphasising that we see it most and best in Browne.
The time was one of great linguistic animation, and
the whole world of English words was in a turmoil.
The language was passing through a violent crisis,
none the less violent because no one seems to have
perceived the fact. Anxious to add a dignity to
English, Browne for his part was all in favour of producing that dignity by a lofty diction founded on
Latin and Greek forms. He thought that we had
neglected our opportunities for the assimilation of
precise and beautiful words. He believed that Latin

was the guard and natural defence of the English language; and in his enthusiasm for the rolling southern music he was certainly inclined to underrate the value of direct and rustic forms of speech.

In a passage of the *Vulgar Errors,* he has let us into his secret thoughts. He says that in writing that book in English, he has deliberately Latinised his vocabulary in order to reach " into expressions beyond mere English apprehensions." He has " declared " himself " in a language best conceived," that is in a language crowded with classical neologisms introduced for the purpose of securing accuracy and subtlety of thought. He goes on to say: " If elegancy still proceedeth, and English pens maintain that stream [of new words] . . ., we shall within few years be fain to learn Latin to understand English, and a work will prove of equal facility in either." This is not set down in ridicule or irony ; it was Browne's conception of " elegancy," of a civilised and perfected English, a language which could only be understood by those who were masters of Latin. This evidence is very precious, for it leaves us in no doubt of Browne's intention, and explains his vocabulary where it becomes so servilely Latin as to be ugly. He had come to the conclusion that classic words were the only legitimate ones, the only ones which interpreted with elegance the thoughts of a sensitive and cultivated man, and that the rest were barbarous. There was a great plausibility in this, but Browne's mistake was to carry it so far as to undermine the integrity of the English language. It was thus that he started that " effectual injury " to the literary taste of the nation which Coleridge deplored.

It is impossible to exculpate Browne from the charge
of using adjectives of classical extraction which are
neither necessary nor natural. There is no excuse
for writing about the "pensile" gardens of Babylon
when all that is required is expressed by "hanging"
gardens. The importance of the nice distinctions that
it is Browne's design to mark, often does not justify
the ugliness of the word he chooses. The disk of the
sun-flower is "honey-combed": then, why say that
it is "favaginous"?   "Paralogical," which scandalised
even Dr. Johnson, is a poor substitute for "unreason-
able."   "Salient" animals are animals that jump;
a webbed object is said to be "interwoven telarly";
we must not explain that things are arranged in a
regular order, but that they "hold a wide uni-
vocacy."   All these examples, it chances, are taken
by turning over the pages of *The Garden of Cyrus*, and
the trick grew upon our author. But even *Religio
Medici* speaks of the "omneity" of God, where "one-
ness" would be simpler and better; and of "oneiro-
criticism" for the interpretation of dreams.

An able and enthusiastic admirer of Browne has
had the courage to defend [1] the whole principle involved
in these creations. To this critic, the phrase in the
Vulgar Errors, "a work desired and yet desiderated,"
so far from seeming redundant, seems "delightful."
To the ear of this partial reader, "digladiation" and
"quodlibetically" are welcome, and even "exantlation" to be tolerated. We follow less breathlessly
when the same modern admirer bids us appreciate
the romantic attraction of sound and novelty in the

---

[1] In the *Times* of December 23, 1904.

phrase "the hill and *asperous* way that leadeth unto
the house of sanity." Here the introduction of a
word like "asperous," although it adds nothing to
the idea of "rough," may be justified by beauty of
sound, but rarely is this the case with Browne's
clumsy audacities. He should have remembered what
Vaugelas, the wisest of all grammarians, said on the
subject of words, that it was commonly far better to
consult women and people who had not studied than
those who are too learnedly oppressed by a knowledge
of Latin and Greek. If that was true for the French,
it was surely still more true for the English, and we
owe no thanks to persons like Browne, who have tried
to make us call man an equicrural animal when all we
mean is that his legs are of a bigness. Browne's rock
ahead is wrapping the trite in the coronation-robes of
fine language.

It is odd that, when he pleases, Browne can be the
most lucid of writers, and employ none but the shortest
and plainest of words. In the very middle of the uplifted peroration of *Urn-Burial* we come upon this
limpid strain of music: —

"Life is a pure flame, and we live by an invisible sun
within us. A small fire sufficeth for life, great flames seemed
too little after death, while men vainly affected precious pyres,
and to burn like Sardanapalus. But the wisdom of funeral
laws found the folly of prodigal blazes, and reduced undoing
fires unto the rule of sober obsequies, wherein few could
be so mean as not to provide wood, pitch, a mourner, and
an urn."

Here the only word that jars upon us is the
Brownesque one, "prodigal."

If he could have kept to this level, and if he had

not been seduced by a certain obscure romance in the
terminology of late Latin writers like Raymond Lully
and Paracelsus, if, too, he could have preserved in
its purity his native instinct for verbal sonority, his
"learned sweetness of cadence," as Pater happily calls
it, no one would have reproached him for his love of
order and decorum, of assonance and alliteration, of
all the curious pomp which he brooded over "in the
areopagy and dark tribunal of his heart." But "exantlation" and "favaginous" lift their ugly faces at
us, and are types of an error in taste which does much
to spoil our pleasure in writings that would else be
almost perfect.

The extravagantly Latinised vocabulary of Sir Thomas
Browne had a direct influence on the style of the eighteenth century, when the expression "Brownism" was
even used to stigmatise excessive Anglo-Latin diction.
This is undoubtedly what Coleridge had in mind; and
this influence rose to its height when Dr. Samuel
Johnson became acquainted with Browne's works,
and permitted them to be one of the models upon
which he "formed his style." It has been lately
said that Boswell's statement that Johnson imitated
Browne must be taken with a grain of salt; but
Boswell knew what he was talking about, and he is
supported by Hawkins. The observation, as Napier
remarked, was made by many of Johnson's contemporaries, and the fact, indeed, was obvious. Moreover,
in 1756, Johnson was drawn by admiration of the
Christian Morals to write on Browne a memoir, which
is one of the most eloquent of his minor writings. In
the course of this memoir, Johnson defines the genius
of Browne, as it displayed itself to him, in words which

are valuable as indicating the point of view accepted
by the greatest critic of the middle of the eighteenth
century: —

" [Browne's] style is, indeed, a tissue of many languages;
a mixture of heterogeneous words, brought together from
distant regions, with terms originally appropriated to one art,
and drawn by violence into the service of another. He must,
however, be confessed to have augmented our philosophical
diction; and, in defence of his uncommon words and expressions, we must consider that he had uncommon sentiments,
and was not content to express in many words that idea for
which any language could supply a single term. But his
innovations are sometimes pleasing, and his temerities happy.
He has many *verba ardentia*, forcible expressions, which he
would never have found, but by venturing to the utmost
verge of propriety, and flights which would never have been
reached, but by one who had very little fear of the shame of
falling."

The earlier part, at least, of this criticism might be
a direct apology for the character of Dr. Johnson's
own style, and we observe with interest that he makes
no reference to the romantic, the imaginative, element
in Browne's diction, this being a matter altogether
outside Johnson's range of perception.   When Browne
says "Man is a noble animal, splendid in ashes and
pompous in the grave, solemnising nativities and deaths
with equal lustre, nor omitting ceremonies of bravery
in the infamy of his nature," he is not talking John-
sonese, good or bad; he is employing his Latinisms to
produce a certain melancholy music which was raised
above Johnson's pitch of hearing.   But the passage
just quoted is taken from *Urn-Burial*, while it is
evident that it was from the later and less romantic
Christian Morals that Johnson took his inspiration.   It

was this work, which is far from being of Browne's
best, which encouraged Johnson, and with him a whole
school of rhetorial writers in the eighteenth century,
to avoid circumlocution by the invention of superfluous
words, learned but pedantic, in which darkness was
concentrated without being dispelled. It was Browne's
misfortune, until his genuine merits were re-discovered
and asserted by Coleridge and Lamb, to serve as a
sort of pattern or excuse to everybody who thrust
a needless Latin idiom upon the language.

If, however, Browne may seem to us to have been
not careful enough of the integrity of the English
language, nor duly sensitive to its proper balance
of elements, his genius was so unique that we hesi-
tate to call what would be crimes in others more
than very venial faults in him. "These crumbling
relics and long-fired particles superannuate such
expectations" may be a sentence which it is impossible to defend as a specimen of pure and nervous
English, but it has its perfect propriety in a solemn
passage of Sir Thomas Browne.   Indeed, it is language
such as this which enables us to comprehend what was
the singular attraction of our writer for Johnson.
Mrs. Thrale, speaking somewhere of the literary taste
of the Lexicographer, says, with witty penetration,
that he liked plate to eat off better than highly-painted
porcelain, meaning that he liked a sumptuous solidity
of style better than mere elegance and dexterity.   In
other words, Browne, with his sonorous weight, pleased
him more than Addison with his precision and delicacy
and brilliant refinement.   In fact, if we allow ourselves
to pursue the image, we can find nothing which suggests
the peculiar art of Browne better than pieces of solid

plate, gold or silver, elaborately chased and stamped
with stately coats of arms, bearing ostensibly the evidences of a lordly habit of life, and fitted for solemn
ceremonial. That these are sometimes heavy in form,
monotonous and yet extravagant in ornament, not suitable for easy household purposes, are defects inherent
in their peculiar quality of pomp.

This solemn and sententious formality grew upon
Browne with the advance of years. We trace it in
Religio Medici, although it is there commonly subdued
to an undertone by the youth and vivacity of the
writer. But in *Urn-Burial* and in *A Letter to a Friend*
it is seen in its full richness; in *The Garden of Cyrus* it
has lapsed into extravagance; and in *Christian Morals*
it has become a mannerism. But in all the works of
Sir Thomas Browne, even in the comparatively colour-
less *Vulgar Errors*, it is there as a central characteristic
of his style, though not always presented to the reader.
Whether the stately movement pleases us now or not
depends entirely upon the amount of emotion which
vibrates through the passage. When Browne is extremely moved by his imagination he can hardly be
too grandiloquent; we accept his most audacious
" Brownisms " with delight. He leads us, at his will,
through his labyrinths of language, and every turn
of the path displays some new sombre beauty, brings
forward to our ears some new strain of melancholy
faëry music.

From these, however, we sometimes break away to
listen to him in a plainer mood. In many of the
pages of *Religio Medici* he writes with as little display
of the buskin, with as little of the dragging robe of
purple, as any one who ever used English as a straight-

forward vehicle for the expression of his thoughts. It
is well that we should turn, from too persistent contemplation of Browne's ecstasies, to such an easy
strenuous example of his personal, his confidential,
manner, as this reflection upon martyrdom, which
reveals so plainly his private emotion : —

" Now, as all that die in the war are not termed soldiers, so
neither can I properly term all those that suffer in matters of
religion, martyrs. The Council of Constance condemns John
Huss for a heretic. The stories of his own party style him
a martyr. He must needs offend the divinity of both, that
says he was neither the one nor the other. There are many,
questionless, canonised on earth that shall never be saints in
Heaven; and have their names in histories and martyrologies,
who, in the eyes of God, are not so perfect martyrs as was
that wise heathen, Socrates, that suffered on a fundamental
point of religion, the Unity of God. I have often pitied the
miserable bishop that suffered in the cause of Antipodes,[1] yet
cannot choose but accuse *him* of as much madness for exposing
his life on such a trifle, as those of ignorance and folly, that
condemned him. I think my conscience will not give me
the lie, if I say there are not many extant that in a noble
way fear the face of death less than myself. Yet, from the
moral duty I owe to the commandment of God, and the
natural respects that I tender unto the conservation of my
essence and being, I would not perish upon a ceremony,
politic points, or indifferency. Nor is my belief of that un-
tractable temper, as not to bow at their obstacles, or connive
at matters wherein there are not manifest impieties. The
leaven, therefore, and ferment of all, not only civil but religious actions, is wisdom, without which, to commit ourselves
to the flames is homicide, and, I fear, but to pass through one
fire into another."

[1] This was Virgilius, Bishop of Salzburg, who is said to have
been burned for believing that there were " a good rascally sort
of topsy-turvy fellows " on the opposite side of the globe.
Browne's sympathy with this prelate is very characteristic.

Few writers are more attractive than Browne to the technical student of literature, since there are few in whom the matter, in its crudest sense, is so completely subordinated to the manner. It is obvious that to Browne the opportunity of producing an æsthetic sensation on the nerves of the reader was the factor which led him to write. He wished to stimulate, perhaps even to dazzle and startle, rather than to instruct his disciples. We may believe the felicities of Jeremy Taylor and the wit of Fuller to have been partly accidental, or at least instinctive, caused by the authors' flights of enthusiasm. We may imagine that these writers did not know how magnificent they were. But Browne, we may be sure, was never carried away. His effects are closely studied, they are the result of forethought and anxious contrivance. We know, from all sources, that he was a very punctilious writer, and he believed that the art of composition was to be learned. We have seen him solicitous that each of his sons should learn it, and all they lacked was just the essential thing, their father's ineffable genius. But he had always worked as though he had no genius at all, with a modest devotion to the principles of the mysterious art of prose.

The result, of course, was that his style was highly artificial ; and those whose passion for simplicity leads them to reject everything that is not slipshod and careless will find nothing in the writings of Sir Thomas Browne to attract them. But readers who are not offended by the evidences of painstaking may find an exquisite pleasure in what Mr. Saintsbury has admirably called the " marquetry " of Browne's style. It is all veneered with the tortoise-shell of his learning,

the stained ivory of his meditations upon life, and it
is not carved out in bold forms, with a chisel or on a
lathe, but, with the daintiest care, fragments, sometimes of no great intrinsic value, are fitted into the
brilliant surface-pattern. It is certain that he had
not the temper of those who cover large spaces with
the creations of their fancy. For this a great liquidity
of mind is required; the imagination must move easily
and rapidly, and wash across wide areas of thought.
There was a certain stagnation of talent in Sir Thomas
Browne. Of a singularly placid and even temper, his
mind was never quite fluid, there was a static element
in it. He liked it to move very gently, to return soon
to the point whence it started, to remain fantastically
controlled and gorgeously reserved.

When he was, as he said, "shaking hands with
delight, in his warm blood and canicular days," he
felt the difficulty, as Montaigne had felt it before him,
of attaining to and retaining the ideal state of moderation. In that extravagant age, it was Browne's great
desire to preserve a delicate comprehension of distinctions. As he grew older, he resigned, perhaps, a
little of the courage with which he started. Beginning
by resolving to ally himself to Christianity, he removed the contest of faith from the ground of reason
and science, and placed it in a mystery. It is very
difficult not to treat the author of *Religio Medici* as a
scoffer, because of his scepticism. But to do so, as we
have attempted to show, is to commit an injustice.
Like Montaigne, once more, and in a fuller sense than
Montaigne, Browne was indignant that a man should
possess a religion " contradictoire à celle qu'il avait en
son cœur." But in process of time, in his moderation

and his scepticism, his own heart became enclosed, not
in a stone, but in a sort of cold crystal. He had never
had, really, Montaigne's passion for truth; and his
religion became a thing which lay there, ostensible
and shining, but holding no communication with his
human sympathy, his imagination or his style.

What inspired Browne to a greater height of
fervour than any other subject was the contemplation
of death. This underlies almost every one of his most
majestic passages. It might be said of him, in a
curious sense, what one of his French contemporaries
declared, " Il nous faut, si nous espérons de parvenir à
quelque gloire, hanter avec les morts." Certainly it is
in the company of those who are " lost in the uncomfortable night of nothing," who " vainly contriving
their bodies in sweet consistencies, to attend the return
of their souls," have found that " all was vanity,
feeding the wind and folly " ; it is in the contemplation
of the millions over whom " the iniquity of oblivion
blindly scattereth her poppy," that Sir Thomas Browne
reaches his most glorious flights of imagination. He
is the laureate of the forgotten dead, of those who had
discovered, what he from the first divined, that this loud
world is nothing but " a dream and a mock-show."
In the presence of a haunting sense of the fragility of
time, of the faint mark we all make on life, something
less durable than the shadow of a leaf or a breath upon
a mirror, Sir Thomas Browne decides that " restless
unquiet for the diuturnity of our memories seems a
vanity almost out of date, and a superannuated piece
of folly." We must do our daily round of duty; we
may polish the bits of intellectual ornament which are
our innocent occasional pastime, we may take refuge

from the sad pressure of infinity in speculation, but to strive and cry, or to exaggerate the importance of things around us, or of ourselves, or of the world itself, would be nothing better than a waste of energy.

If we take this view of the temperament of Sir Thomas Browne, we need feel no surprise that his actual performance, from the scholar's point of view, was curiously inadequate to what we must suppose to have been his ambitions. These were encyclopædic, or rather may have been, for we know not what it was that he placed before himself as his aim in life. His accumulated knowledge, however, was not allowed to crush him. He shrank, indeed, from the excessive labours which, alike in science and literature, bow a man to the earth with a composite sense of the infinitude of nature and his own infirmity. Browne sighs, faintly, for more leisure; laments, conventionally, the pressure of professional duties. But he does not express these discomforts as Bacon or as Selden might. He does not chafe against the disability, he does not view the arrival of a messenger from a patient's bedside with vexation and alarm. We have the feeling that such fragments as he has left us — and all his books are fragments — occupied him lightly, were easily concluded, satisfied the literary craving through months and even years of inactivity. Attention has been called in an earlier part of this memoir to the fact that once, through the year 1658, when he had reached the age of fifty-three, he was roused to active production and to something of the excitement with which a poet pours out his lyrical verses in full enthusiasm. But this mood sank immediately, and if we except the compositions of

that year, what have we? We have a charming
fragment of mental autobiography, an incomplete
criticism of some wide fields of natural history, an
episode in the career of a physician, and some desultory jottings on ethics.

In spite of this, it would be an error to consider the
Norwich doctor as an amateur in literature. If his
works are few, and fragmentary, it seems to be because
he concluded that the manner of saying a thing was
all-important, and because he could often compress
the entire splendour of his art within a small compass.
We must admit that if this was his theory, he was
justified in it. He is said to have dreamed for forty
years about a continuation of *Religio Medici*; but could
he have recaptured the delicate charm of adolescence,
could he have added to our gratified approval of his
adroitness? If he had given a dozen clinical experiences in detail, would they have increased our admiration of the penetrative skill shown in *A Letter
to a Friend*? One find of rough pots at Walsingham
inspired a masterpiece in *Urn-Burial*; would a vast
tome on the antiquities of Norfolk have been anything
but a disappointment to us? And if we could discover that he had composed the huge *thesaurus* on
horticulture of which there was talk in his correspondence with Evelyn, should we be willing to exchange
for it the last brief chapter of *The Garden of Cyrus*?
Browne's medical experience had made him keenly
aware of the small horizon of human life, and it is
difficult to believe that he did not consciously restrict
himself to the creation of a few matters which should
be exquisite, and his own, and self-sufficing.

INDEX

A

Account of Island, alias Iceland, 146.

Acetaria (Evelyn), 131.

Aldrovandi, Ulisse (Pontifex Maximus), 77, 78, 81, 83, 87.

Amyot, Thomas, v.

Anthony à Wood, 5.

Anthropometamorphosis (Bulwer), 190.

Arcadia (Sannazaro), 22 *n.*

—— (Sidney), 22 *n.*

Arcana Microcosmi (Ross), 100.

Arcanum of Hermetic Philosophy (Dee), 136.

Aristotle, 70, 74, 81.

Ashmole, Elias, 136, 137.

B

Bacon, Dr. Arthur, 80 *n.*

—— Sir Edmund, of Redgrave, 121, 148.

—— Nicholas, 121, 122, 132, 167.

—— Francis, 52, 72, 73, 75.

Bagford, John, 176.

Bates, Henry, 63.

Benlowes, Edward, 63.

Bentley, Richard, 19.

Boyle, Robert, 153.

Brampton Urns, 174.

Broadgates Hall (Oxford), 4.

Browne, Anne, 159, 160.

—— Dorothy. *See* Dorothy Mileham.

—— Dr. Edward, 7, 19, 59, 60,

82 *n.*, 144-6, 151, 155-7, 158-9, 163, 164, 167, 188-9.

Browne, Richard, 3.

—— Sir Thomas, pedigree, 1-2; 1 *n.*; parentage, 2; grandparents, 2, 3, 4; alternative spelling of name, 2 *n.*; infancy, 2-3; death of father, 3; stepfather, 4, 5; youth, 4-24; gains scholarship at Winchester, 4; graduates from Pembroke (Broadgates Hall), 4, 5; his tutor, 4-5, 23; travels in France and Italy, 7; attitude towards foreign habits and customs, 8; studies at Montpellier, 10-12; at Padua, 12-15; at Leyden, 15-16; takes medical degree there, 16; advantages gained intellectually, 16-17; returns to England, 18; resides at Halifax, 19; incorporated doctor of physic at Oxford, 23; marriage, 24; children, 24, 141; education of, 140-1; their adoration for him, 141; advice to sons, 142, 143, 151; fame as a physician, 24, 148; his creed, 28; love for small things, 34-5, 86; love of nature, 35, 71; superstition, 39, 73; ideas on resurrection of the body, 42; on hell and eternal punishment, 43-4; opinion of himself, 47; European fame, 60; disciples, 63, 100, 104, 106, 108; religious

209